2026
중등영어 교사임용

재미와 실력을 동시에,

중등영어

이동걸 영어학

기출문제분석

통사론

음운론

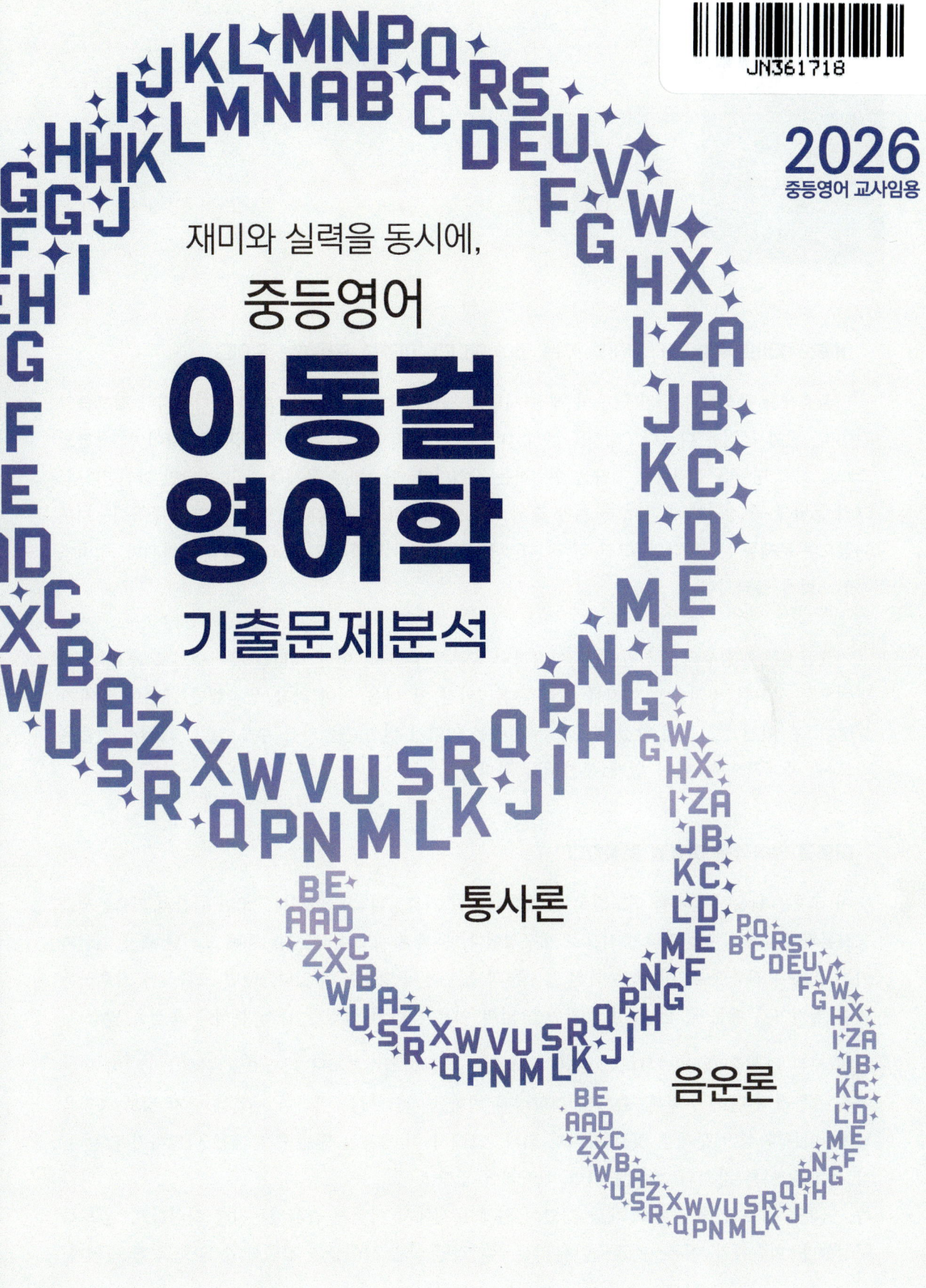

서 문
Preface

기출분석이란 무엇인가: 과거를 푸는 것이 아니라, 미래를 준비하는 일이다

기출문제를 분석한다는 건 단순히 예전 시험 문제를 푸는 게 아니다. 그건 어디까지나 겉모습일 뿐이다. 진짜 목적은 다르다. 기출을 분석한다는 건 곧 출제자의 두뇌를 해킹하는 일이며, 수험생 스스로 학습 방향을 점검하고 전략을 수립하는 작업이다. 단순하게 문제를 풀고 정답만 확인한다면, 그건 두뇌 운동 정도에 그친다. 하지만 출제 의도를 예측하고, 출제자가 어떤 개념에 주목했는지를 되짚으며 문제를 분석한다면, 그건 전략이다. 학습의 깊이가 달라지고, 사고의 방식이 바뀌며, 성적은 자연스럽게 올라간다.

기출문제는 수험생의 나침반이다. 어디까지 공부해야 할지, 어떤 개념을 우선순위로 둘지, 어떤 방식으로 사고를 정리해야 할지를 알려준다. "이건 안 나올 거야"라고 생각했던 개념이 갑자기 등장하고, "이건 중요하지 않겠지"라고 무시했던 영역이 변별력을 가를 수도 있다. 그래서 기출은 반드시, 체계적으로, 깊이 있게 분석해야 한다.

이동걸 영어학은 이렇게 분석한다

이 교재는 단순히 문제를 연도별로 정리해 나열한 기출정리집이 아니다. 20여 년간의 기출문제를 통사론과 음운론의 이론영역 중심으로 재구성했다. 문제 자체보다, 문제를 통해 드러난 출제 패턴과 이론 흐름에 집중했다. 이 책은 특히 통사론과 음운론에 방점을 두었다. 매년 고득점을 좌우하는 핵심 영역이기 때문에, 단순 정답 확인을 넘어 이론 기반의 정밀한 문제 분석에 초점을 맞췄다.

이 모든 분석은 2002년부터 2025년까지의 기출문제 전수조사를 바탕으로 한다. 20년이 넘는 기출 흐름을 면밀히 추적해, 출제의 경향성과 변화를 파악했다. 이러한 자료는 단지 정보 축적을 넘어, 이론과 실전 문제를 잇는 다리가 된다. 그래서 이 교재는 단순히 문제를 나열하지 않는다. 각 문항은 이론 강의의 흐름에 따라 배열되어 있다.
즉, 이론을 공부한 후 곧바로 해당 개념이 실제 문제에서 어떻게 출제됐는지를 확인할 수 있도록 구성했다. 학습자가 '이론→기출→이해'라는 유기적인 학습 사이클을 경험할 수 있도록 한 것이다.

수강생이 해야 할 일은?

분석은 문제를 푼 다음에 더 큰 의미가 있다. 적어도 각 소단원의 문제는 미리 풀고, 각 문항의 출제 의도를 스스로 추론해 보자. 정답을 맞췄더라도, 그 이유가 '운'이었는지 '이해'였는지 구분해야 한다. 자신이 헷갈린 포인트를 표시하고, 예시답안과 비교하면서 논리 흐름을 점검하자. 그리고 반드시, 다시 한번 써 보자. 답안을 다시 쓰는 것, 그것이 바로 사고 구조를 정리하는 최고의 훈련이다. 복습도 그냥 읽는 게 아니다. 연관 개념을 묶어서 정리하고, 혼동하기 쉬운 개념은 비교해 암기해야 한다. 시험장에서 시간을 절약해 주는 건 이런 반복적 정리와 숙달이다.

기출은 과거가 아니다. 그것은 가장 믿을 수 있는 미래 예고서다.
그렇다면, 예고서를 그냥 넘기지 말고 분석하자. 출제자의 손보다 먼저 움직이는 사람이, 결국 합격하는 법이다.

2025년 7월

이동걸

목 차

Contents

PART Ⅰ

통사론 6

CHAPTER 01 **Lexicon** 7

CHAPTER 02 **Phrases** 19

CHAPTER 03 **Binding Theory** 69

CHAPTER 04 **Case Theory** 81

CHAPTER 05 **Control Theory** 89

CHAPTER 06 **Movements** 93

PART Ⅱ

음운론 114

CHAPTER 01 Phonetics & Phonology 115

CHAPTER 02 Allophonic Rules 127

CHAPTER 03 Phonological Process 143

CHAPTER 04 Syllable 189

CHAPTER 05 Stress 203

CHAPTER 06 Foot 217

CHAPTER 07 Intonation 225

PART I

통사론

CHAPTER

01

Lexicon

영역	출제년도	내용
1. Subcategoization		
2. Selection restriction	2002-전국18	Selectional restriction
3. Argument Structure		
4. Thematic relation	2024-A13	Theta-role
	2025-B5	Theta-criterion
5. Types of Intransitives	2017-A12	Unergative/Unaccusative
6. Passivization		
7. Expletives	2012(2차)-01	‘there’ and ‘here’

❑ 연도별 출제빈도

2002	2003	2004	2005	2006	2007	2008	2009	2010	2011	2012	2013	2014	2015	2016	2017	2018	2019	2020	2021	2022	2023	2024	2025	2026
*										*					*							*	*	?

1. 다음을 읽고, 물음에 답하시오. 【3 points】 2002-전국18

> The yellow fog that <u>rubs</u> its back
>   upon the window-panes,
> The yellow smoke that <u>rubs</u> its muzzle
>   on the window-panes,
> <u>Licked</u> its tongue in the corners of the evening,
> <u>Lingered</u> upon the pools that stand in drains,
> …

위의 예문들의 의미상 변칙적(anomalous)이나 비유적 표현으로 쓰이고 있다. 이런 쓰임을 밑줄 친 동사들의 주어 선택제약(selectional restriction)과 관련하여 설명하시오.

출제 영역

Lexicon 〉 Selectional restriction

출제 의도

시에서 사용된 비유적 표현은 의미상 변칙적(anomalous)이다. 즉 어휘의 속성 중 하나인 선택제약을 위반한다. 술어가 논항인 주어에게 어떠한 선택제약을 가하고 시에서 사용된 주어가 의미적으로 어떻게 선택제약을 위반하는지 말할 수 있어야 한다.

문제 풀이 과정

동사 'rubs', 'licked', 'lingered'의 의미는 각각 '문지르다', '핥다', '머물다'이다. 이들 동사의 주어자리는 동사의 행위를 할 수 있는 개체가 위치해야한다. 하지만, the yellow fog, the yellow smoke는 그런 행위를 할 수 없다. 그래서 변칙적이다. 그렇지 않으면 비유적인 의미로 사용될 수 있다.

풀이 과정에서 어려운 점

선택제약문제를 풀기 위해서는 동사의 의미를 반드시 알아야 한다.

답안

The underlined verbs impose a semantic restriction on their subjects. That is, the subject of the verbs should denote an entity that is able to 'rub', 'lick', and 'linger'. but the subject can't. Thus, the expressions can be used only in a figurative sense.

과제

핵심개념과 관련 부분 읽어 보세요

- selectional restriction : 트포 p.369
- anomaly (형용사 anomalous)
- arguments: 트포 p.371

2. Read the passage and fill in each blank with ONE word from the passage. Write your answers in the correct order. 【2 points】 2024-A13

> Every predicate is associated with an argument structure, which specifies the number of arguments it requires. The predicate assigns its arguments thematic roles including the following:
>
> - Agent: the instigator of the action
> - Theme: the entity affected by the action or state
> - Experiencer: the entity experiencing the psychological state
> - Instrument: the means by which the action or event is carried out
>
> Thematic roles do not have a one-to-one relationship with grammatical functions such as the subject, the object, and so on. For example, the argument *the ball* is the object in (1a) and the subject in (1b), but it retains the same thematic role, Theme, in both sentences. Other examples can be seen in (2).
>
> (1) a. David kicked the ball.
> b. The ball was kicked by David.
>
> (2) a. A brick smashed the window.
> b. They expected the ship to sink.
> c. David opened the door slowly.
> d. Bob cut the tree with a saw.
>
> The subject in (2a) and the object of the preposition in (2d) carry the role of ___①___, whereas the subject of the subordinate clause in (2b) and the object in (2c) have the role of ___②___.

출제 영역

Lexicon 〉 Thematic role

출제 의도

술어는 논항에게 의미역을 할당한다. 논항이 받는 의미역을 말할 수 있어야 한다. 기초적인 개념을 묻는 문제이다.

문제 풀이 과정

의미역은 주어나 목적어같은 grammatical function과 연결되지 않는다. 따라서 논항의 의미역을 확인하기 위해서는 문장의 전체의미를 살펴봐야한다. 아래 (a)와 (d)에서 밑줄 친 논항은 동사의 행위의 도구이다. 따라서 도구역(instrument)을 갖는다.

a. A brick smashed the window.

d. Bob cut the tree with a saw.

하지만, (b), (c)에서 밑줄 친 논항은 동사의 행위의 대상이 되므로 대상역(Theme)을 할당 받는다.

b. They expected the ship to sink.

c. David opened the door slowly.

풀이 과정에서 어려운 점

답안

instrument, theme

과제

핵심 개념과 관련 부분 읽어보세요.

- thematic role : '트포' ch.7 (7.10 Thematic relations), 'Syntax' ch.8 2.Thematic Relations and Theta Roles
- argument structure : 트포 p.382

3. Read the passage in 〈A〉 and the examples in 〈B〉, and follow the directions. 【4 points】

2025-B5

It is well-known that predicates can take different numbers of obligatory arguments. For example, a transitive predicate like *hit* requires two arguments—a subject and an object—and a ditransitive predicate like *put* requires three arguments—a subject, a direct object, and an objective predicative complement.

(1) a. Bill hit the ball.
    b. Bill put the violin on the table.

One way to encode these restrictions is to use thematic relations, where each argument receives a specific theta-role assigned by the verb. For instance, in (1a), *hit* assigns an agent theta-role to *Bill* and a theme theta-role to *the ball.* This thematic relation can be represented formally in a structure called a theta-grid. The theta-grid for *hit* is as follows:

(2) Hit 〈<u>Agent NP</u>, Theme NP〉

To ensure that a sentence is grammatical, two conditions must be met: (i) each argument must receive only one theta-role, and (ii) each theta-role must be assigned to only one argument. This requirement is known as the theta-criterion. Object relative clauses introduce an intriguing pattern: A relative pronoun can either appear or remain silent, as seen in the following example:

(3) John met the man (who) Mary kissed.

It is assumed that the relative pronoun *who* originally appears in the object position of the relative clause and moves to the front of the embedded clause (i.e., Spec CP), as shown in (4a). Its silent counterpart that corresponds to the relative pronoun, marked $\varnothing_{wh}$, is assumed to follow the same process as in (4b).

(4) a. John met the man $[_{CP}$ who $[_{TP}$ Mary kissed $t_{wh}]]$.
    b. John met the man $[_{CP}$ $\varnothing_{wh}$ $[_{TP}$ Mary kissed $t_{wh}]]$.

Note: 't_{wh}' indicates the trace of the wh-word and its silent counterpart, $\varnothing_{wh}$.

(a) *Susan put the book.
(b) *The ball John hit it broke the window.

Note: '*' indicates the ungrammaticality of the sentence.

Based on 〈A〉, explain why (a) and (b) in are ungrammatical, respectively, in terms of the theta-criterion.

출제 영역

Lexicon 〉 Theta Criterion

출제 의도

의미역 기준(theta criterion)을 이해하고 있는지 묻고 있다. 다음과 같은 두 개의 기준을 각각 적용할 수 있어야 한다. (i) each argument must receive only one theta-role, and (ii) each theta-role must be assigned to only one argument. 〈B〉박스에 두 문장을 제시한 것도 각각 위반한 의미역기준이 다르다는 것을 의미한다. 또한 보이지 않는 관계대명사도 동사의 논항이 될 수 있다는 점을 유의해야 한다.

문제 풀이 과정

A박스 요약 및 핵심내용

1. 술어의 논항구조 (논항갯수) 설명
2. 의미역을 논항에 할당하는 방식 설명하고 theta-grid로 그 방식을 표현한다.
3. 의미역 할당 조건인 의미역기준 theta criterion 설명
4. 관계대명사가 '보이는' 관계대명사와 '보이지 않는 silent' 관계대명사로 표현될 수 있다는 점을 언급한다.
   (관계대명사가 silent하더라고 기저 생성된 자리에서 의미역을 받는 논항이라는 것을 말하고자 함)

B박스 분석 과정

B박스의 두 문장이 비문인 이유를 theta criterion으로 설명해야 한다.

(a) *Susan put the book. (b)*The ball John hit it broke the window. 이 두 문장은 모두 의미역기준을 위반하여 비문이다. 하지만 각각 설명을 달리해야 한다. (a)와 (b) 두 문장을 우리에게 제시한 이유가 바로 그것이다. 이 것을 서로 다르게 설명하려면 theta criterion (i)과 (ii)차이를 정확하게 알아야 한다. 첫 번째 조건은 의미역을 받지 못하는 논항이 있어서는 안 된다는 점을 강조하며, 두 번째 조건은 술어의 의미역이 모두 할당되어야지 하나라도 할당되지 않는 경우가 있어서는 안 된다는 점을 지적한다. 문장 (a)는 put이 할당해야 하는 의미역 세 개중 두 개만 할당되고 하나는 할당하지 못했기 때문에 (ii)위반이고, (b)는 의미역을 할당 받지 못하는 논항 it이 존재하므로 (i)의 위반이다. 이 두 조건의 차이점을 정확하게 구분해야 한다.

풀이 과정에서 어려운 점

Theta Criterion의 두 조건을 별도로 적용할 수 있어야 한다.(많이 혼동됨)

답안

In (a), 'put' is a ditransitive verb that requires three arguments, but only two are provided, with no argument available to receive a theta role, which violates the second condition of the theta criterion. In (b), 'hit' is transitive, assigning thematic roles to 'John' and a silent relative pronoun. The pronoun 'it' cannot receive a thematic role, violating the first condition of the theta-criterion.

과제

핵심개념과 관련 자료 읽어보세요.

- 의미역기준: 트포 p.391, Syntax p.249
- 관계대명사절 구조: 트포 p.493

4. Read the passage in 〈A〉 and the sentences in 〈B〉, and follow the directions. 【4 points】

2017–A12

Not all intransitive verbs are of the same kind. Compare the two sentences in (1) and (2).

(1) An angel jumped on the hill.
(2) An angel appeared on the hill.

Although both of the above sentences are intransitive, they are not of the same kind. They have different syntactic and semantic properties. In (1), the subject originates in the specifier position external to the V–bar constituent, receiving an Agent role. Verbs like *jump* are known as unergative verbs. However, in (2), the superficial subject originates in the complement position within the immediate V–bar projection of the verb, receiving a Theme role. Then it moves to subject position. Verbs like *appear* are known as unaccusative verbs.

The two types of intransitive verbs can be distinguished by means of tests such as the following. Unaccusative verbs like *appear* allow a word order called *there* inversion, where the underlying complement remains in its original position after the verb. On the other hand, since the subject of unergative verbs like *jump* does not originate in the complement position of the verbs, it isn't allowed to appear in that position after the verbs with *there* inversion, as shown below.

(3) *There jumped an angel on the hill.
(4) There appeared an angel on the hill.

Note: * indicates that the sentence is ungrammatical.

(i) Several people ate in the Korean restaurant.
(ii) Several customers shopped in the new shopping center.
(iii) Several students remained in the school library.
(iv) Several soldiers saluted in the military ceremony.
(v) Several complications arose in the medical experiment.

Identify the TWO sentences containing an unaccusative verb in 〈B〉, and explain the reason by using the test described in 〈A〉.

출제 영역

Lexicon 〉 Intranstives

출제 의도

자동사의 유형을 구분하고 각 유형의 특징을 묻는 문제이다. 자동사의 주어가 어디서 생성되었고 무슨 의미역을 할당받았는지 알고 있어야 한다.

문제 풀이 과정

A박스 요약 및 핵심내용

아래 문장은 표층적 구조는 동일하지만 도출과정이 다르다. (1)에서 jumped의 주어는 'the specifier position external to the V-bar constituent'에서 생성된다. 즉 주어자리에서 생성된다. 그리고 Agent의미역을 할당받는다. 하지만 (2)에서 appeared주어는 'the superficial subject originates in the complement position within the immediate V-bar projection of the verb'에서 생성된다. 즉, 동사 뒤에서 생성되고 theme의미역을 할당받는다.

(1) An angel jumped on the hill.
(2) An angel appeared on the hill.

(2)에서 주어는 동사뒤에서 생성되므로 주어자리에 there가 위치할 수 있다.

(3) *There jumped an angel on the hill.
(4) There appeared an angel on the hill.

B박스 분석 과정

아래에서 unaccusative 동사는 NP에 Theme의 의미역을 할당하므로 주어가 Theme인 것을 찾으면 된다. (iii)과 (v)에서 주어가 theme의미역을 가지므로 unaccusative이다. 그리고 이 두 구문은 there inversion구문으로 표현될 수 있다.

(i) Several people ate in the Korean restaurant. (Agent)
(ii) Several customers shopped in the new shopping center. (Agent)
(iii) Several students remained in the school library. (Theme)
(iv) Several soldiers saluted in the military ceremony. (Agent)
(v) Several complications arose in the medical experiment. (Theme)

풀이 과정에서 어려운 점

'remain'같은 동사의 주어가 theme 의미역을 갖는다는 점을 잘 알아야 한다.

답안

Sentences (iii) and (v) contain an unaccusative verb: 'remained', 'arose'. The subject NPs of the verbs receive a theme role, not an agent role, and there inversion is allowed as follows: (iii) There remained several students in the school library. (v) There arose several complications in the medical experiment.

과제

핵심 개념과 관련 내용을 공부하세요.

- ergative & unaccusative verbs
  - '트포' 8.6 NP movement in ergative and middle structures,
  - 'Syntax' ch11_6 Inherently Passive verbs: Unaccusatives
- Thematic role
- NP-movement

5. Read the passage and follow the directions. 2012(2차)-01변형

> Sentences in (1) are both grammatical.
>
> (1) a. There will be a big tennis match on Friday afternoon.
>   b. Here will be a big tennis match on Friday afternoon.
>
> (2) a. There will be a big tennis match on Friday afternoon, won't there?
>   b. Here will be a big tennis match on Friday afternoon, won't here?

State which sentence in (2) is grammatical, and then discuss why, based on the characteristics of the expletive there.

출제 영역

Lexicon 〉 Expletives

출제 의도

허사 there는 항상 주어자리에 위치하고 주어로 역할을 한다는 점을 알아야 한다. 문장의 가장 앞자리가 항상 주어자리가 아니다. 도치현상에 의해 주어가 아닌 요소가 문두에 위치할 수 있기 때문이다. 따라서 주어의 지위를 tag question을 통해 확인할 수 있다.

문제 풀이 과정

(1)에서 there과 here가 문두에 위치하지만 (1a)의 there은 허사로서 주어자리에 위치하지만 (1b)는 도치구문으로 here는 주어가 아니다.

(1) a. There will be a big tennis match on Friday afternoon.
 b. Here will be a big tennis match on Friday afternoon.

위 주장을 증명하기 위해 tag question으로 만들면 (2b)는 비문이된다. tag의 'won't here'에서 here은 주어가 아니므로 그 자리에 위치할 수 없다.

(2) a. There will be a big tennis match on Friday afternoon, won't there?
 b. Here will be a big tennis match on Friday afternoon, won't here?

풀이 과정에서 어려운 점

답안

The sentence (2a) is grammatical. Tag question are made using an auxiliary verb and a subject pronoun. The expletive 'there' occur in the subject position, and can be used as a subject pronoun in the tag question, but the demonstrative 'here' is not a subject.

과제

핵심 개념과 관련 자료 학습하세요.

- Expletives 'there'
- Tag questions
- subjecthood

CHAPTER

02

Phrases

영역		출제년도	내용
1. Ambiguity		2007-전국24 / 2023-A07	Two modifiers
		2011-30	Structural Ambiguity
		2015-A04	Lexical/Structural Ambiguity
		2018-A09 / 2024-B05	Scope Ambiguity
2. Constituency Tests		2006-전국07 / 2014-A04	
3. Categories		2023-B02	'there' and 'fast'
		2005-전국24	'whether' and 'if'
4. X-bar Theory	4.1 Complement/Adjunct	2003-전국15	'English Teacher'
		2003-전국16	'claim that ... '
		2006-서울인천21-22	
		2008-전국15	
		2022-A07	'Korean professor'
		2009-27	one-substitution
		2009-32	'of'-PP
		2010-36	구조적 차이
		2016-B06	
		2021-A03	preposition vs postposition
	4.2 Specifier	2020-B01	position of 'all'
	4.3 Head		
	4.4 Categorial Status		
5. Clauses	5.1 Ordinary Clause (CP)	2021-B05 / 2018-A12	CP vs TP
	5.2 Exceptional Clauses (TP)	2007-전국16	ECM vs PRO
	5.3 Small Clause (SC)		

❑ 연도별 출제빈도

2002	2003	2004	2005	2006	2007	2008	2009	2010	2011	2012	2013	2014	2015	2016	2017	2018	2019	2020	2021	2022	2023	2024	2025	2026
	*		*	*	**	*	**	*	*			*	*	*		*			*	*	*		*	?

1. 〈A〉의 밑줄 친 문장은 (a)~(d)의 구조로 해석될 수 있다. 〈B〉의 (1)과 (2)가 보여 주는 상황이 (a)~(d) 중에서 어떤 구조로 해석된 것인지 각각 그 기호와 이유를 쓰시오. 【3 points】

2007-전국24

<u>The cowboy rode the horse from the town with spirit.</u> (a) *with spirit* modifies the NP headed by *town* and *from the town* modifies the NP headed by *horse.* (b) *with spirit* modifies the NP headed by *town* and *from the town* modifies the VP headed by *rode.* (c) *with spirit* modifies the NP headed by *horse* and *from the town* modifies the NP headed by *horse.* (d) *with spirit* modifies the VP headed by *rode* and *from the town* modifies the NP headed by *horse.*

(1) With spirit, the cowboy rode the horse that was from the town. (2) The cowboy rode the horse away from the town that had spirit.

출제 영역

Phrases > Ambiguity

출제 의도

두 개의 수식어구로 인해 네 가지 유형의 수식이 발생하는 문장을 제시한다. 각 수식 방식에 따른 의미를 파악할 수 있어야 한다.

문제 풀이 과정

네 가지 수식 방식을 나타내는 수형도를 그려보고 구조적 차이점과 각 구조의 의미를 파악해야 한다.

'The cowboy rode the horse from the town with spirit.
PP1 PP2

풀이 과정에서 어려운 점

답안

(d) is related to the sentence (1) since 'with spirit' modifies the VP and 'from the town modifies the NP 'horse'. (b) is related to the sentence (2) since 'with spirit' modifies the NP 'town' and 'from the town modifies the VP headed by 'rode'.

과제

각 수식방식의 따른 의미를 영어로 paraphrasing 하는 연습을 하자. 중의성문제는 대부분 그 의미를 답안에 내가 작성해야 하기 때문이다.

2. Read the passage in 〈A〉 and the examples in 〈B〉, and follow the directions. 【4 points】

2023-A7

A sentence sometimes allows for more than one reading when a modifier has more than one option to take. For instance, in (1) the PP *in France* may modify a verb to derive the meaning of "I went to France where a seminar on language took place," or a noun to derive the meaning of "The seminar was about language in France."

(1) I went to a seminar on language in France.

In syntax, branches are not allowed to cross in tree structure, which is also known as the No Crossing Branches (NCB) constraint. Observe that sentence (2a) is ruled out, and its ungrammaticality is attributed to a violation of the NCB constraint, as shown in (2b).

(2) a. *The baby might be afraid in the park of new people.

b.

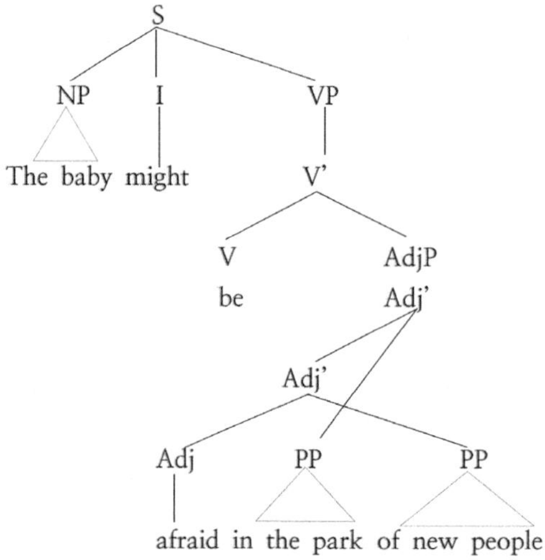

Note: '*' indicates the ungrammaticality of the sentence.

(3) The man is talking to the woman with a tablet on the desk.

a. The man is on the desk, and the woman owns a tablet.
b. The woman is on the desk, and the man owns a tablet.
c. The woman owns a tablet, and the tablet is on the desk.

(4) a. He should not surely break his promise.
b. He should surely not break his promise.
c. He surely should not break his promise.

Note 1: Assume that *surely* is a sentence adverb adjoining to the S node.
Note 2: Assume that *not* merges at Spec VP in tree diagrams.

Based on 〈A〉, first, identify the ONE structurally unavailable reading in (3) in 〈B〉 and identify the ONE ungrammatical sentence in (4) in 〈B〉, both of which violate the NCB constraint. Second, explain how the sentence you chose in (4) violates the NCB constraint.

출제 영역

Phrases 〉 Ambiguity

출제 의도

수식요소가 여러 개 등장할 때 어느 요소를 수식하는 정확하게 알아야 하고 더불어 수형도로도 표현할 수 있어야 한다.

문제 풀이 과정

A박스 요약 및 핵심내용

1. (1) 'I went to a seminar on language in France' 두 의미:
   a. the PP *in France* may modify a verb : 'I went to France where a seminar on language took place'
   b. the PP *in France* may modify a noun : 'The seminar was about language in France.'

2. No Crossing Branches (NCB) constraint : branches are not allowed to cross in tree structure
   (Adjunct 'in the park'이 complement 'of new people'를 선행하면 branches가 cross되어 비문임)
   (2) a. *The baby might be afraid in the park of new people.

B박스 분석 과정

(3) The man is talking to the woman with a tablet on the desk.
   a. The man is on the desk, and the woman owns a tablet.
   b. The woman is on the desk, and the man owns a tablet.
   c. The woman owns a tablet, and the tablet is on the desk.

▶ (b)처럼 'on the desk'가 woman을 수식하고, 'with a tablet'이 man을 수식한다면 branches가 cross됨

(4) a. He should not surely break his promise.
   b. He should surely not break his promise.
   c. He surely should not break his promise.

▶ Note에서 surely가 문장부사로 S node에 첨가되고, *not* 은 Spec VP에 위치한다는 점을 참고해야 한다. 즉, not이 surely보다 선행할 수 없다는 것을 구조적으로 이미지화 할 수 있어야 한다. 따라서 (4a)가 비문이다.

풀이 과정에서 어려운 점

surely가 문장부사로 S node에 첨가되고, *not* 은 Spec VP에 위치한다는 점만 구조적으로 이미지화 할 수 있다면 쉽게 풀 수 있는 문제이다.

답안

The sentence (3b) has a structurally unavailable reading, and the sentence (4a) is ungrammatical. In (4), the sentence adverb 'surely' is within the VP, and in order for it to adjoin to the S node, it has to cross a branch.

과제

- 문장 (1)에서 중의성을 야기하는 두 구조를 수형도로 그려보세요.
- (3)과 (4)문장을 수형도로 그려보세요.

3. Read 〈A〉 and 〈B〉 and follow the directions. 【2 points】 2011-30

Structural ambiguity results when more than one phrase-structure tree can be assigned to a sentence. In other words, if the sentence is associated with more than one surface structure representation. it is structurally ambiguous (e.g., *The father of the boy and the girl will travel to India.*). Here the sentence can be associated with two different surface structure representations. In one representation, only one person, the father, will travel. In the other representation, two people will travel: the girl and the father of the boy.

a. Mrs. Coleman gave her dog biscuits this morning.
b. My brother told the teacher that he ran into something.
c. Who do you think Jim believes Judy wants to meet the mayor?
d. The boys have been waiting for more than an hour by the bank.
e. Under no circumstances are passengers permitted to open the doors.
f. The pilot said that flying airplanes is really dangerous.

Based on 〈A〉, choose all and only the sentences in 〈B〉 that are structurally ambiguous.

① a, b
② a, b, f
③ a, c
④ c, d, e
⑤ c, d, f

출제 영역

Phrases 〉 Ambiguity

출제 의도

구조적 중의성을 갖는 문장을 고르는 단순한 문제이다. 어휘적 중의성은 배제시켜야 하고 'flying airplaines'은 중의성이 없다는 점까지 확인해야 한다.

문제 풀이 과정

- 아래 (a)는 [$_{NP}$ her] [$_{NP}$ dog biscuits]이거나 [$_{NP}$ her dog] [$_{NP}$ biscuits]의 구조를 갖는다.
  a. Mrs. Coleman gave her dog biscuits this morning.
- 아래 (b)는 told의 complements로 [$_{NP}$ the teacher] [$_{CP}$ that he ran into something], 또는 [$_{NP}$ the teacher that he ran into] [$_{NP}$ something]의 구조를 가질 수 있다.
  b. My brother told the teacher that he ran into something.
- 문장 (f)에서 'flying airplanes'은 이 자체로 구조적 중의성을 갖지만 이 문장 속에서는 중의성이 없다. is의 단수형은 '날아가는 비행기들'이 아닌 '비행기를 날리는 것'으로만 해석되기 때문이다.
  f. The pilot said that flying airplanes is really dangerous.

풀이 과정에서 어려운 점

- (b)이 두 개의 문장 구조로 나타낼 수 있다는 점을 빨리 파악해야 한다.
- (f)에서 'flying airplanes'이 '날아가는 비행기들'로 해석될 수 없다는 점을 빨리 파악해야 한다.

답안

①

과제

중의성이 있는 문장(a)와 (b)의 두 의미를 각각 영어로 써보자.

4. Read the passage in 〈A〉 and the sentence in 〈B〉, and follow the directions. 【5 points】

2015-A04

> Linguistic expressions are often ambiguous, and homonymy is one source of ambiguity. Homonyms are words that have different meanings but are pronounced the same, and may or may not be spelled the same. Another source of ambiguity is structure. Sometimes, homonymy creates even more ambiguity in combination with different structures.
>
> (1) John admires intelligent professors and students.
> (2) They are pitchers from America.
> (3) Mary observed the man at the bank.
>
> The ambiguity in (1) is created by different structures. The source of the ambiguity in (2) is homonymy, whereas (3) is ambiguous due to different structures and homonymy.

> Mary saw John's nose ring.

Identify the source(s) of the ambiguity of the sentence in 〈B〉. Then explain why the sentence is ambiguious and write the two readings of the sentence.

출제 영역

Phrases 〉 Ambiguity

출제 의도

어휘적 중의성과 구조적 중의성을 파악할 수 있어야 하고 이 두 유형의 중의성이 결합할 때 다양한 중의성이 발생할 수 있다.

문제 풀이 과정

A박스 요약 및 핵심내용

(1) John admires intelligent professors and students. (Structural Ambiguity) – intelligent의 수식구조에 따라 중의성 발생

(2) They are pitchers from America. (Lexical Ambiguity) – pitchers의 두 의미 '항아리'와 '투수'

(3) Mary observed the man at the bank. (Structural and Lexical Ambiguity) – at the bank의 수식 구조와 bank의 두 의미 '은행'과 '강둑'

B박스 분석 과정

Mary saw John's nose ring.에서 [$_{NP}$ John's nose] [$_{VP}$ ring] 구조와 'ring'이 코를 골다의 의미로 해석된다. 또한 [$_{NP}$ John's nose ring]구조와 'ring'이 코의 악세사리 의미로 해석된다.

풀이 과정에서 어려운 점

중의성 문제는 두 개의 의미를 영어로 정확하게 표현하는것이 어렵다. (가끔 답안에 작성한 그 의미도 중의성이 있는 경우가 많다.)

답안

(b) is ambiguous due to different structures and homonymy. The first reading is that Mary saw John's nose pendant, which is created when 'John's nose ring' is considered as an NP and 'ring' a noun meaning a pendant. The second reading is that Mary saw John snoring when 'John's nose ring' is considered as a small clause and 'ring' a verb meaning 'snore'

과제

문제의 구조적 중의성 있는 문장들을 수형도로 그려보자.

5. Read the passage and follow the directions. 【4 points】 2018-A09

There are expressions that are ambiguous because of scope interaction between a quantifier and another quantifier or between a quantifier and a negative expression. Consider the following sentences.

(1) a. Every boy likes a girl.
    b. Every student respects a professor.

Sentence (1a) and sentence (1b) are ambiguous because *every boy* and *every student* can have a wide scope over *a girl* and *a professor*, and *a girl* and *a professor* can have a wide scope over *every boy* and *every student*, respectively.

(2) a. Every student has not done their assignment.
    b. I have not eaten all the cookies.

In (2a) and (2b), *every student* and *all the cookies* can have a wide scope over *not*, and *not* can have a wide scope over *every student* and *all the cookies*.

Sentence (3) below is ambiguous. Write TWO possible meanings of the sentence and state how its ambiguity can be explained in terms of scope interaction.

(3) Mary refused to visit every city that Tom visited.

출제 영역

Phrases > Ambiguity (Scope Ambiguity)

출제 의도

한 문장에 양화사가 두 개가 존재하거나 양화사와 부정어가 존재한다면 이들 간의 영역으로 인해 중의성이 발생한다. 영역 차이로 인해 발생하는 두 의미를 영어로 표현할 수 있어야 한다.

문제 풀이 과정

A박스 요약 및 핵심내용

(1) a. Every boy likes a girl.

- Every boy > a girl : 'a girl'이 총칭으로 해석. 즉, 각 소년이 다른 한 명의 소녀를 좋아한다.
- a girl > Every boy : 'a girl'을 특칭으로 해석. 특정한 한 소녀를 모든 소년이 좋아한다.

(2) a. Every student has not done their assignment.

- Every (or All) > not : 전체부정
- not > Every (or All) : 부분부정

B박스 분석 과정

'Mary refused to visit every city that Tom visited.' (refuse = not accept 의미이므로 negative expression이 포함된다.)

- every > not : 모든 도시를 방문하지 않음
- not > every : 일부 도시 방문

풀이 과정에서 어려운 점

양화사로 인한 scope 중의성은 두 개의 의미를 작성하는 것이 어렵게 느껴진다. (많은 연습이 필요하다)

답안

Sentence (3) can have two meanings. First meaning is that Mary did not visit any city that Tom visited. The other meaning is that Mary might visit some of the cities that Tom visited. If the quantifier *every* has a wide scope over the word *refused*, the sentence has the first interpretation, whereas if it has a narrow scope, the sentence has the second interpretation.

과제

- Quantifier movement로 인해 Scope가 달라지므로 이 이동에 대해 공부해 둔다.
- 영역 차이로 인한 중의성 의미를 모두 영어로 작성해 본다.

6. Read the passage and follow the directions. 【4 points】 2024–B5

> The scope of negation is the part of the sentence that the negative applies to semantically. Scope is best understood by examining the ambiguity of (1) as shown in (2):
>
> (1) The editor did not find many mistakes in the paper.
>
> (2) a. The editor is not very good, and although there were many mistakes he did not find them.
>
> b. The editor searched thoroughly for mistakes, but the paper did not have many mistakes in it.
>
> When we express the variations in meaning using scope, in (2a) we have a situation where many has scope over the negative: *many* 〉 *not*. By contrast, in (2b), the negative has wide scope over *many*: *not* 〉 *many*.
>
> The scope interpretation is also found with the negative and an adverb. In (3), the negative and the adverb show different relations pertaining to scope, each of which reflects the linear order at surface structure.
>
> (3) a. I did not omit my name deliberately.
>
> b. I deliberately did not omit my name.
>
> In (3a), the negative has scope over the adverb (*not* 〉 *deliberately*): omitting my name was not something I made a point of doing. In (3b), however, the adverb has scope over the negative (*deliberately* 〉 *not*): I made a point of not omitting my name.
>
> However, the scope interpretation does not always conform to the linear order at surface structure as in (3). Consider in (4) the two modal auxiliaries, expressing deontic necessity, in relation to the negative.
>
> (4) a. You must not tell anyone about it.
>
> b. You need not tell anyone about it.

Based on the passage, state which word has scope over the other for each sentence in (4). Then describe the meaning of each sentence using the structural frame 'necessary that.'

출제 영역

Phrases 〉 Ambiguity (Scope Ambiguity)

출제 의도

양화사와 부정어, 부정어와 부사의 상호작용, Modal과 부정어의 상호관계를 이해하고 그것을 'necessary that' 구조로 문장을 작성할 수 있어야 한다.

문제 풀이 과정

1. not과 quantifier의 상호작용으로 인한 중의성
'The editor did not find many mistakes in the paper.'

- many 〉 not의 의미

   a. The editor is not very good, and although there were many mistakes he did not find them.

- not 〉 many의 의미

   b. The editor searched thoroughly for mistakes, but the paper did not have many mistakes in it.

2. not과 adverb의 상호작용으로 인한 중의성

- not 〉 deliberately

   a. I did not omit my name deliberately. (omitting my name was not something I made a point of doing)

- deliberately 〉 not

   b. I deliberately did not omit my name. (I made a point of not omitting my name.)

3. not과 auxiliary와 상호작용이 어순과 관련 있는 것은 아니다. (a)의 must not '~하지 말아야 한다'의미로 must 〉 not의 영역을 갖는다. 하지만 'need not'은 '~할 필요 없다' 의미이므로 not 〉 need 영역을 갖는다.

   a. You must not tell anyone about it. → It is necessary that you do not tell anyone about it.
   b. You need not tell anyone about it. → It is not necessary that you tell anyone about it.

풀이 과정에서 어려운 점

- must not...과 need not...의 의미를 정확하게 알아야 한다.
- 마지막 (4)의 문장들에 관한 내용과 이에 대한 디렉션을 정확하게 이해해야 한다. (이 부분이 정확하게 무엇을 어떻게 하라고 하는건지 모르는 경우가 있으면 안된다.)

답안

In (4a), the modal 'must' has scope over the negative, meaning that 'it is necessary that you do not tell anyone about it'. In (4b) the negative has scope over the modal 'need', meaning that 'it is not necessary that you tell anyone about it'.

과제

중의성이 있는 문장은 반드시 다양한 의미를 영어로 직접 작성해봐야 한다. 위 문제에 언급된 중의적 문장의 의미를 스스로 직접 작성해 보자.

7. 〈A〉를 읽고, 구성 성분 테스트(constituent test)를 이용하여 〈B〉에 주어진 문장의 밑줄 친 부분이 구성 성분(constituent)이 될 수 있는지 없는지를 설명하시오. 【4 points】 2006-전국07

Consider the sentence below

(1) John will meet his employer at the castle.

(2) a. At the castle, John will meet his employer.
b. His employer, John will meet at the castle.
c. Meet his employer at the castle, John will (indeed).

(3) a. *Employer at the, John will meet his castle.
b. *Meet his, John will employer at the castle.

In each of the sentences in (2) a group of words has been moved to the beginning of the sentence, since it forms a syntactic unit called a constituent. On the other hand, in (3), the preposed words do not form constituent. That is why they are ungrammatical. Only a constituent can be preposed.

① The people can move <u>the sculpture into the museum</u>.
② The people can see <u>the sculpture from the museum</u>.

출제 영역

Phrases 〉 Constituency Tests

출제 의도

구성 성분 테스트(constituent test)를 이용하여 구성 성분(constituent)이 될 수 있는지 없는지를 설명할 수 있어야 한다.

문제 풀이 과정

A박스 요약 및 핵심내용

- Only a constituent can be preposed.

(3)의 'Employer at the'와 'Meet his'는 구성성분이 아니므로 preposing될 수 없다.

a. *Employer at the, John will meet his castle.
b. *Meet his, John will employer at the castle.

B박스 분석 과정

성분테스트를 이용하여 밑줄 친 부분이 구성성분인지 판단하라고 하지만, 문제에 접근하는 순서는 밑줄 친 부분이 구성성분임을 먼저 파악해야 한다.

① The people can move the sculpture into the museum.

▶ PP 'into the museum'은 move를 수식하므로 'the sculpture into the museum'은 구성성분일 수 없다. 따라서 preposing한다면 비문이 된다.

② The people can see the sculpture from the museum.

▶ 박물관에서 온 조각상이란 의미이므로 PP 'from the museum'은 sculpture를 수식한다. 따라서 the sculpture from the museum은 구성성분이고 preposing한다면 정문이 된다.

풀이 과정에서 어려운 점

문미의 PP가 어디를 수식하는지 해석을 통해 파악해야 한다.

답안

The underlined words in ① is a constituent since the elements cannot be moved into the beginning of the sentence. However, the underlined words in ② can form a constituent since they can be preposed like 'The sculpture from the museum, the people can see.'

과제

〈B〉의 두 문장의 수형도를 그려보자. (PP의 수식관계에 유의해서 그려야 한다.)

8. Read the passage in 〈A〉 and the sentences in 〈B〉, and follow the directions. 【4 points】

2014–A04

A constituent is a string of one or more words that syntactically and semantically behaves as a unit. The constituency of a string of words can be verified by a number of constituency tests, two of which are *movement* and *substitution*.

(1) Can you confirm your receipt of my application for membership? (2) Call the reviewers of Bill's new book in a week. (3) The music festival was crowded with young composers of jazz from Asia. (4) Tina bears a striking resemblance to her mother.

Choose all the sentences where the underlined part qualifies as a constituent and identify the syntactic category of each constituent. Then explain how movement and/or substitution can be applied to verify the constituency of each string of words.

출제 영역

Phrases 〉 Constituency Tests

출제 의도

〈B〉의 문장에서 밑줄 친 표현이 구성성분인지 알아야 하고 그것이 구성성분이라면 무슨 범주적 지위를 갖는지 말할 수 있어야 한다. 더불어 해당 구성성분을 이동과 대체 테스트를 통해 증명할 수 있어야 한다. 실질적으로 이 문제를 풀기 위해서는 specifier, complement, adjunct를 구분할 수 있고 구조적 측면도 이해해야 접근할 수 있다.

문제 풀이 과정

A박스 요약 및 핵심내용

1. 구성성분의 정의 : A constituent is a string of one or more words that syntactically and semantically behaves as a unit.
2. 구성성분 테스트 : movement, substitution

B박스 분석 과정

밑줄 친 부분이 specifier까지 포함하고 있는지 확인해야 한다. 만약 그것을 포함하고 있다면 NP 전체가 밑줄이 있어야 구성성분이 될 수 있다. 만약 N을 수식하는 PP가 포함되지 않는다면 구성성분이 될 수 없다. 밑줄 친 부분이 specifier까지 포함하지 않는다면 N-bar 범주만으로도 구성성분이 될 수 있으므로 문장 뒤 PP가 N의 complement인지 adjunct인지 따져봐야 한다. 더불어 문장 뒤 PP가 N의 수식요소인지 문장의 동사를 수식하는 건지도 따져봐야 한다.

(1) Can you confirm <u>your receipt of my application</u> for membership?

▶ Specifier 'your'가 존재하므로 application을 수식하는 PP 'for membership'까지 포함되어야 구성성분이 될 수 있다. 'for membership'은 complement이므로 반드시 포함되어야 한다.

(2) Call <u>the reviewers of Bill's new book</u> in a week.

▶ Specifier 'the'가 존재하고 NP 전체에 밑줄이 있으므로 구성성분이다. 이 때 PP 'in a week'은 동사 call을 수식하므로 NP와 상관없는 요소이다.

(3) The music festival was crowded with <u>young composers of jazz</u> from Asia.

▶ Specifier가 없다. 따라서 from Asia가 명사 composers를 수식하는 요소이지만 adjunct이므로 밑줄에 포함되지 않아도 구성성분(N-bar범주)이 될 수 있다.

(4) Tina bears <u>a striking resemblance</u> to her mother.

▶ Specifier 'a'가 존재하므로 resemblance을 수식하는 PP 'to her mother'까지 포함되어야 구성성분이 될 수 있다. 또한 'to her mother'은 complement이므로 반드시 포함되어야 한다.

풀이 과정에서 어려운 점

- 문장 뒤 PP가 수식하는 곳이 어디며 또한 complement인지 adjunct인지 구분해야 한다.
- (3)에서 밑줄 친 부분이 N-bar범주라는 것을 주의해야 한다.

답안

The underlined part of (2) and (3) is a constituent, an NP and N', respectively. The NP in (2) can be replaced with the pronoun 'him' like 'Call them in a week.' The N-bar constituent in (3) can be replaced with the proform 'ones' like 'The music festival was crowed with young composers of Jazz from Asia, and ones from Europe.'

과제

(1)~(4)문장의 수형도를 그린 후 구성성분 여부를 눈으로 확인해 보자.

9. Read the passages in ⟨A⟩ and ⟨B⟩, and follow the directions. 【2points】 2023-B2

Traditionally the parts of speech such as adjective, adverb, noun, preposition, or verb have been defined under semantic criteria. For example, nouns are defined as words that denote people, things, animals, and places. In many cases, the traditional definition works well as *teachers, tables, cats,* and *schools* are all categorized as nouns. However, there are many other cases in which the definition does not work. For instance, *sincerity, love,* and *destruction* are all nouns but they denote a personality trait, an emotional state, and a process, respectively.

As an alternative, syntacticians categorize the parts of speech under distributional criteria. They group words that can fit in the syntactic context and then name the category. In the distributional context in (1), for example, words such as *dog, child, analysis,* or *love* can fill in the blank, but other words like *in, eliminate,* or *sadly* can't; in other words, no part of speech other than a noun can occur in the blank.

(1) His ________ is great.

Bearing the description above in mind, consider the following examples in (2) – (5) that show the distributions of *there* and *fast*.

(2) a. They repaired the car right there.
b. *They repaired the car right fast.
c. They repaired the car right in that building.

(3) a. They repaired the car very fast.
b. *They repaired the car very there.
c. They repaired the car fast enough.
d. *They repaired the car there enough.

(4) a. The people there are very cheerful.
b. *The people fast are very cheerful.
c. The people at work are very cheerful.

(5) a. The place he drove his car to is in the center.
b. *The place he drove his car to is fast.
c. The place he drove his car to is there.

Note: '*' indicates the ungrammaticality of the sentence.

Under distributional criteria, we can draw a conclusion that *there* should be counted as a(n) ①________ functioning as the head of its own phrase and *fast* as a(n) ②________ functioning as the head of its own phrase.

Fill in the blanks ① and ② in ⟨B⟩ each with ONE word from ⟨A⟩, in the correct order.

출제 영역

Phrases 〉 Categories

출제 의도

품사의 의미적 정의가 아닌 분포적으로 이해하고, there과 fast를 분포적 측면에서 품사를 말할 수 있어야 한다.

문제 풀이 과정

A박스 요약 및 핵심내용

1. 품사의 의미적 정의 및 문제점

Nouns are defined as words that denote people, things, animals, and places. *Sincerity, love,* and *destruction* are all nouns but they denote a personality trait, an emotional state, and a process, respectively.

2. 품사의 분포적 정의

Words such as *dog, child, analysis,* or *love* can fill in the blank, but other words like *in, eliminate,* or *sadly* can't; in other words, no part of speech other than a noun can occur in the blank.

(1) His _____ is great.

3. Distributions of *there* and *fast*.

B박스 분석 과정

(2) a. They repaired the car right there.
b. *They repaired the car right fast.
c. They repaired the car right in that building.

(c)에서 'right'은 P의 수식어구이다. 'there' 앞은 가능하지만 'fast'앞을 불가능 → 'there'은 전치사!

(3) a. They repaired the car very fast.
b. *They repaired the car very there.
c. They repaired the car fast enough.
d. *They repaired the car there enough.

(a)와 (c)에서 fast는 부사자리에 위치하고 very와 enough로 수식받지만, there은 불가 → 'fast'은 부사!

(4) a. The people there are very cheerful.
b. *The people fast are very cheerful.
c. The people at work are very cheerful.

(c)에서 명사 people뒤 전치사구가 위치하듯이 (a)의 there 가능 → 'there'은 전치사!

(5) a. The place he drove his car to is in the center.
b. *The place he drove his car to is fast.
c. The place he drove his car to is there.

(a)에서 is 뒤 전치사구가 위치한 것처럼 (c)에서 there 위치 가능 → 'there'은 전치사!

풀이 과정에서 어려운 점

- 품사를 의미적으로 정의하는 것이 우리에게 더 익숙한 반면, 분포적으로 분석하는 건 익숙치 않다.
- (2)~(4)의 데이터가 말하고자 하는 것을 정확하게 이해해야 한다.

▶ [용어정리] parts of speech

답안

preposition, adverb

과제

품사뿐만 아니라 주어나 목적어같은 문법적 기능요소들의 의미적 정의/분포적 정의를 구분하여 정리해보자. ('트포' 참조)

10. 다음 〈A〉를 읽고, 지시에 따라 답하시오. 【6 points】 2005-전국24

> Traditional grammarians have classified *whether* and *if* as the same grammatical category, i.e.., subordinate conjunction. If we look at the two grammatical sentences below, it might seem as if there is a potential parallelism between *whether* and *if*, since they appear to occupy the same position.
>
> I don't know *whether* he will come here.
> I don't know *if* he will come here.
>
> Do *whether* and *if* actually belong to the same grammatical category? There are arguments that *whether* and *if* belong to different grammatical categories.

다음 〈B〉의 문장을 읽고, (1) 비문법적인 문장을 모두 찾아 그 기호를 쓰시오. (2) whether, if가 의문부사(wh-adverb)와 같은 문법 범주에 속하는지, 아니면 보문소(complementizer) that과 같은 문법 범주에 속하는지, 주어진 자료에 기초하여 쓰고, (3) 그 판단의 통사적 근거를 쓰시오.

> (a) I wonder whether to go.
> (b) I wonder if to go.
> (c) I wonder when to go.
> (d) I wonder that to go.
>
> (e) I'm not certain about whether he'll come here.
> (f) I'm not certain about if he'll come here.
> (g) I'm not certain about when he'll come here.
> (h) I'm puzzled at that he should have resigned.
>
> (i) I don't know whether or not he will turn up.
> (j) I don't know if or not the will turn up.

출제 영역

Phrases 〉 Categoreis

출제 의도

주어진 데이터를 분석하여 whether과 if의 문법 범주가 의문부사인지 아니면 보문소(complementizer)인지 말할 수 있어야 한다.

문제 풀이 과정

A박스 요약 및 핵심내용

whether과 if의 범주:

1. 전통적 정의 : 접속사(subordinate conjunction) 즉, '의문부사' (우리에게 익숙한 정의임)
2. 문제제기 : 과연 whether과 if가 동일한 범주일까?

B박스 분석 과정

(a) I wonder whether to go.
(b) *I wonder if to go.
(c) I wonder when to go.
(d) *I wonder that to go.

whether은 when과 같이 to go와 함께쓰이지만
if와 that은 불가
→ whether과 if는 서로 다른 범주!

(e) I'm not certain about whether he'll come here.
(f) *I'm not certain about if he'll come here.
(g) I'm not certain about when he'll come here.
(h) *I'm puzzled at that he should have resigned.

전치사 about뒤에 whether과 when은 가능하지만
if와 that은 불가능
→ whether과 if는 서로 다른 범주!

(i) I don't know whether or not he will turn up.
(j) *I don't know if or not the will turn up.

whether은 or not과 함께 쓰일 수 있지만 if는 불가능함
→ whether과 if는 서로 다른 범주!

풀이 과정에서 어려운 점

주어진 문장을 통해 whether과 if의 차이점을 분석하기 위해서 문법성이 구분되어야 하는데 이 문제는 그 문법성을 이미 내가 판단해야 한다는 점에서 부담스럽다.

답안

(b), (d), (f), (h) and (j) are ungrammatical. 'Whether' belongs to the same category as wh-adverbs, since 'whether' and wh-adverbs have infinitival clause as in (b) and (d), since they can function as a complement to a preposition like 'about' as in (f) and (h). However, 'if' cannot go with an infinitival clause. function as a complement to a preposition, and go with 'or not'

과제

11. Read the passage and follow the direction. 【4 points】 2003-전국15

> Consider the following two dialogues:
>
> (1) A: Do you like the English teacher?
> B: Yes, I do. He's French, but he teaches English so well.
>
> (2) A: Do you like the English teacher?
> B: Yes, I do. He's a typical Englishman. But interestingly, he teaches Spanish, not English.
>
> The two different stress patterns are associated with two different meanings. Let's assume that just as each N-bar in a sentence is a semantic unit, so too each N-bar is a phonological unit.

The meanings of 'English teacher' in the conversation (1) and (2) are different. State why they are different readings, based on their structures and stress pattern.

출제 영역

Phrases 〉 X-bar Theory

출제 의도

'English teacher'에서 'English'가 complement인지 adjunct인지 맥락을 통해 분석할 수 있어야 한다. 구조적 관계를 정확하게 알아야 stress pattern 물음에 답할 수 있다.

문제 풀이 과정

1. (1)의 'English Teacher'에서 'English'의 기능

(1) A: Do you like the English teacher?
B: Yes, I do. He's French, but he teaches English so well.

▶ '그는 프랑스인이지만 영어를 가르친다'는 B의 답변에서 English는 과목이므로 complement이다.

2. (2)의 'English Teacher'에서 'English'의 기능

(2) A: Do you like the English teacher?
B: Yes, I do. He's a typical Englishman. But interestingly, he teaches Spanish, not English.

▶ '그는 영국인이지만 스페인어를 가르친다'라는 B의 답변에서 English는 영국인을 의미하므로 Adjunct이다.

3. 'English'의 두 의미와 강세 패턴

Each N-bar in a sentence is a semantic unit, so too each N-bar is a phonological unit.

▶ (1)의 English는 Complement이므로 'English Teacher'는 하나의 N-bar에 관할되므로 하나의 의미, 하나의 강세 패턴을 갖는다. 하지만 (2)의 English는 Adjunct이므로 'English Teacher'는 두 개의 N-bar로 구성되므로 두 개의 의미 단위와 두 개의 강세 패턴을 갖는다.

풀이 과정에서 어려운 점

의미 차이로 인한 Complement/Adjunct 구분과 각 의미에 맞는 구조를 정확하게 알아야 한다.

답안

'English' in (1) is a complement since 'the English teacher' means someone who teaches English. However, 'English' in (2) is an adjunct since 'the English teacher' means 'a teacher who is English'.

과제

(1)과 (2)에서 English Teacher의 구조를 의미에 맞게 그려 보세요.

12. Consider the sentences below and follow directions. 【5 points】 2003-전국16

(1)	a.	the claim that the proof was false
	b.	the claim that John is a genius
(2)	a.	the claim that John has made
	b.	the claim that John found upsetting

State structural differences between the sentences (1) and (2)

출제 영역

Phrases > X-bar Theory

출제 의도

명사를 수식하는 'that'절 (CP)이 Complement인지 Adjunct인지 구분할 수 있어야 한다.

문제 풀이 과정

(1) a. the claim that the proof was false
b. the claim that John is a genius

▶ (1)에서 that절은 claim의 내용을 말하므로 claim과 의미적으로 밀접한 관련성을 갖는다. 따라서 complement 이다.

(2) a. the claim that John has made
b. the claim that John found upsetting

▶ (1)에서 that절은 claim을 한정하는 의미로 사용되므로 claim과 의미적으로 밀접한 관련성이 없다. 따라서 Adjunct이다.

풀이 과정에서 어려운 점

답안

In (1), that-clause is a complement of the head 'claim' since it is used as an appositive. However, that-clause in (2) is an adjunct since it is used as a restrictive relative clause.

과제

- (1)과 (2)의 표현들을 수형도로 그려보자.
- Relative clause에서 wh-movement가 적용되는 과정을 정리하자 (카니 'Syntax'참고)
- Wh-movement의 이동제약으로 Complex NP constraint를 정리하자. (카니 'Syntax'참고)

13. Read the passage and follow the directions. 2006-서울인천21-22

> Consider the underlined noun phrases below:
>
> (1) a. Mr. Smith is a teacher of children.
>   b. Mr. Smith is a teacher from America.
>
> (2) Mr. Smith is a teacher of children from America.
>
> The noun phrase in (2), which is a combination of (1a) and (1b), is ambiguous. The phrase *from America* modifies either the head *teacher* or the head *children*. Thus, the ambiguity results from the possible modification of either head by the phrase *from America*.
>
> However, with the intended meaning 'Mr. Smith teaches children and he is from America,' sentence (3) is ungrammatical:
>
> (3) *Mr. Smith is a teacher from America of children.
>
> The notions of complement and adjunct can be used to explain the ungrammaticality of (3). A complement is a phrase required by the head while an adjunct is its optional modifier; *from America* is an adjunct of the head *teacher* and *of children*, its complement. The noun phrase in (3) is ungrammatical since it does not satisfy the structural requirement that the ______ should come closer to the head than the ________ does.

Fill in each blank with ONE word from the passage. And the underlined verb phrase below is also ambiguous. State two meanings and explain why they have different meanings, based on the structure of the phrase.

> The student read the book on the stool.

출제 영역

Phrases > X-bar Theory >Complement vs Adjunct

출제 의도

수식어가 어디를 수식하는지 정확하게 파악해야 하고 그로 인한 구조적 중의성을 알아야 한다.

문제 풀이 과정

A박스 요약 및 핵심내용

1. Noun 수식하는 PP modifier

(1) a. Mr. Smith is a teacher of children.
b. Mr. Smith is a teacher from America.

2. Structural Ambiguity

The phrase *from America* modifies either the head *teacher* or the head *children*:

(2) Mr. Smith is a teacher of children from America.

With the intended meaning 'Mr. Smith teaches children and he is from America,' sentence (3) is ungrammatical:

(3) *Mr. Smith is a teacher from America of children.

3. Complement vs Adjunct ordering

The noun phrase in (3) is ungrammatical since it does not satisfy the structural requirement that the complement should come closer to the head than the adjunct does.

B박스 분석 과정

'The student read the book on the stool.'

▶ PP 'on the stool'이 read를 수식할 수 있고. book을 수식할 수 있다. 첫 번째 read를 수식할 때 의미는 'The student read the book sitting on the stool.'이고, 두 번째 book을 수식할 때는 'The student read the book that is put on the stool.'의미를 갖는다.

풀이 과정에서 어려운 점

중의적인 문장의 의미를 작성할 때 의미가 정확하게 구분되도록 작성해야 한다.

답안

complement, adjunct

The first reading is that the student read the book sitting on the stool when the PP 'on the stool' modifies the VP. However if the PP 'on the stool' modifies the noun 'book', the meaning is that the student read the book that is put on the stool.

과제

Mr. Smith is a teacher of children from America.와 'The student read the book on the stool.'를 의미에 따라 수형도를 그리보세요.

14. 글 〈A〉를 읽고 〈B〉에서 비문법적인 문장을 찾아 기호를 쓰고, 비문법적인 이유를 〈A〉에 나오는 용어를 이용하여 쓰시오. 【4 points】 2008-전국15

X-bar theory is a very simple and general theory of phrase structure. Using only three rules, this theory accounts for the distinction between adjuncts, complements, and specifiers.

(1) a. Specifier rule: XP → (YP) X'
b. Adjunct rule: X' → X' (ZP) or X' → (ZP) X'
c. Complement rule: X' → X (WP)

X is a head, WP is a complement, ZP is an adjunct, and YP is a specifier. Let us think, here, about differences between the complement and adjunct rule. Because the complement rule introduces the head, the complement will always be adjacent to the head. Or more particularly, it will always be closer to the head than an adjunct. This is seen in the following tree.

(2)

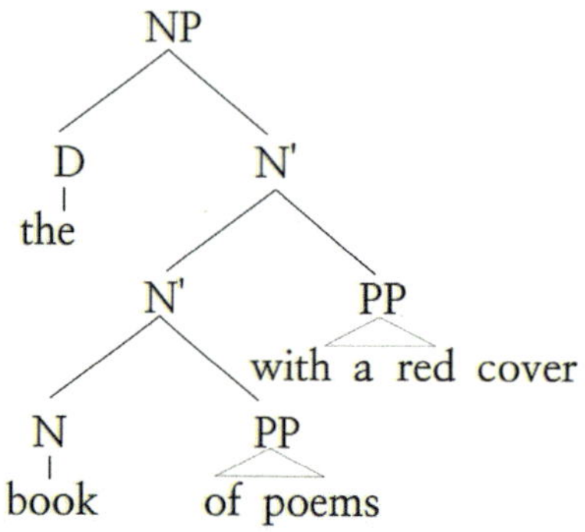

Since the adjunct rule takes an X' level category and generates another X' category, it will always be higher in the tree than the output of the complement rule. Since lines can't cross, this means that complements will always be lower in the tree than adjuncts, and will always be closer to the head than adjuncts.

(a) It is very interesting and of great help.
(b) The flower moved of itself and with elegance.
(c) She likes the book of poems and from The MIT Press.
(d) I read the book of poems with a red cover and with a blue spine.

출제 영역

Phrases 〉 X−bar Theory 〉 Complement vs Adjunct

출제 의도

complement와 adjunct를 구분할 수 있어야 하고 그 구조적 차이점도 정확하게 파악해야 한다.

문제 풀이 과정

A박스 요약 및 핵심내용

1. Distinction between adjuncts, complements, and specifiers.

(1) a. Specifier rule: XP → (YP) X'
b. Adjunct rule: X' → X' (ZP) or X' → (ZP) X'
c. Complement rule: X' → X (WP)

(2)

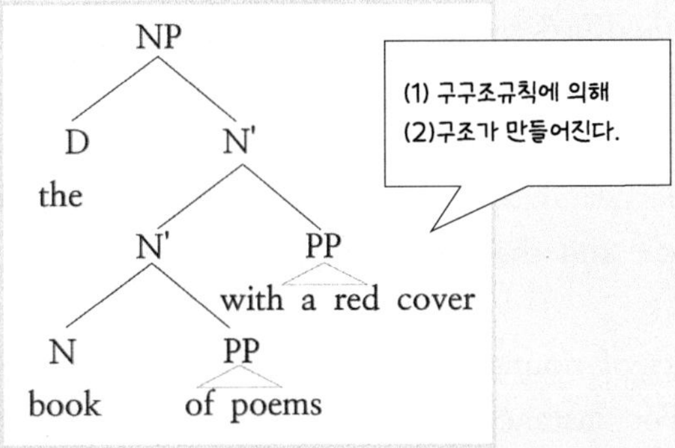

Since lines can't cross, this means that complements will always be closer to the head than adjuncts.

B박스 분석 과정

- Complement와 Adjunct를 구분하고 이들은 서로 Coordination 불가능하다.
  (a) It is [very interesting] and [of great help]. 'is'의 complement끼리 coordination됨. 정문
  (b) The flower moved [of itself] and [with elegance]. 'move'의 Adjunct끼리 coordination됨, 정문
  (c) She likes the book [of poems] and [from The MIT Press]. complement와 adjunct가 연결, 비문
  (d) I read the book of poems [with a red cover] and [with a blue spine]. adjunct끼리 연결, 정문

풀이 과정에서 어려운 점

coordinaton된 성분들의 기능을 알면 쉽게 접근할 수 있음.

답안

The sentence (c) is ungrammatical. The PP 'of poems' is a complement of the noun 'book' and the PP 'from The MIT Press' is an adjunct. A complement cannot be coordinated with an adjunct as in (c).

과제

지문의 (1) PS-rule을 암기하세요.

15. Read the passage and follow the directions. 【4 points】 2022-A07

> Coordination is possible when two constituents share the same type of syntactic function. As shown in (1a), a complement can be conjoined by another complement. If it is combined with an adjunct, however, ungrammaticality results as in (1b).
>
> (1) a. We won't reveal [$_{\text{Complement}}$ the nature of the threat] or[$_{\text{Complement}}$ where it came from].
>
> b. *I went [$_{\text{Complement}}$ to the park] and [$_{\text{Adjunct}}$ for health reason].
>
> The syntactic function of dependents (i.e., complements or adjuncts) influences one-replacement of nouns, too. Note, for example, that a noun prince can be replaced by one in (2a), but not in (2b). The difference lies in what syntactic function the PP serves in each example. The noun is modified by an adjunct in (2a), but by a complement in (2b).
>
> (2) a. The prince from Denmark and the one from Japan met each other yesterday.
>
> b. *The prince of Denmark and the one of Japan met each other yesterday.
>
> It is possible for dependents of nouns to appear in a pre-nominal position, which triggers structural ambiguity. For instance, Korean in 'the Korean professor' can be interpreted as either complement or adjunct: the professor teaching the Korean language and the professor from Korea, respectively.
>
> *Note*: '*' indicates the ungrammaticality of the sentence.

> (i) The man who entered the room was the linguistics and Korean professor.
>
> (ii) Mina is not the Japanese professor but the Korean one.

Based on 〈A〉, identify in whether Korean in (i) and (ii) should be interpreted as language, nationality, or both. Write your answers in the correct order. Then, explain your answers on the basis of the description in 〈A〉.

출제 영역

Phrases 〉 X-bar Theory 〉 One-substitution

출제 의도

complement와 adjunct를 구분할 수 있어야 하고, 이를 기초로 구조적 차이점과 one 대체 현상을 설명할 수 있어야 한다.

문제 풀이 과정

A박스 요약 및 핵심내용

1. Coordination

A complement can be conjoined by another complement. If it is combined with an adjunct, however, ungrammaticality.

(1) a. We won't reveal [$_{Complement}$ the nature of the threat] or[$_{Complement}$ where it came from].
b. *I went [$_{Complement}$ to the park] and [$_{Adjunct}$ for health reason].

2. One-replacement

One is modified by an adjunct in (2a), but by a complement in (2b).

(2) a. The prince from Denmark and the one from Japan met each other yesterday.
b. *The prince of Denmark and the one of Japan met each other yesterday.

3. Pre-nominal modifier

It triggers structural ambiguity. For instance, Korean in 'the Korean professor' can be interpreted as either complement or adjunct: the professor teaching the Korean language and the professor from Korea, respectively.

B박스 분석 과정

(i) The man who entered the room was the <u>linguistics</u> and <u>Korean</u> professor.
▶ Korean은 linguistics과 coordination되었으므로 language로 해석되고 complement이다.

(ii) Mina is not the Japanese professor but the <u>Korean</u> one.
▶ one은 오직 adjunct에 의해 수식받는다. 따라서 Korean은 adjunct이므로 nationality로 해석된다.

풀이 과정에서 어려운 점

답안

(i) language, (ii) nationality; In (ii), 'linguistics' is a complement, which can be conjoined by another complement, 'Korean.' In (ii) the noun 'professor' can be replaced by 'one', which means that the noun is modified by an adjunct.

과제

- (i)의 Korean professor와 (ii)의 Japanese professor의 수형도를 그려보자.
- One 대체에 관한 기출문제 '2009-27' 문제를 분석해 보자.

16. Read 〈A〉 and 〈B〉 and follow the directions. 【2 points】 2009-27

〈A〉

The pronouns *one* and *it* are used to refer to nominal expressions. However, they are not only semantically but also syntactically different. Thus, students may misuse them unless they understand their usage. This means that teachers need to have a good knowledge of the principles governing pronominal usage in order to teach their students how to use the pronouns correctly. In relation to their syntactic characteristics, *one* can replace an N' (not an N), while *it* can replace an NP.

〈B〉

A: I bought a book in this bookstore yesterday.
B: What kind of book did you get?
A: It's a book of poems with a pink cover by Wordsworth.
B: Is it interesting?
A: Yes, very interesting. Why don't you buy a poetry book too?
B: Yes, I'd like to. But I'd like to buy a modern ⓐ one by a different author.
A: Which ⓑ one?
B: I'd like to get a book of poetry by T. S. Eliot.
A: How about that ⓒ one over there?
B: Do you mean the ⓓ one of poetry with a yellow cover?
The book on the top shelf?
A: Yes, ⓔ one with a green-colored spine just next to the poetry book by Frost.

Choose all the INCORRECT uses of one in 〈B〉 based on 〈A〉.

① ⓐ, ⓑ
② ⓐ, ⓒ
③ ⓑ, ⓒ
④ ⓒ, ⓓ
⑤ ⓓ, ⓔ

출제 영역

Phrases 〉 X-bar Theory 〉 One-substitution

출제 의도

One이 N-bar성분을 대체한다는 점을 알아야 한다. 이것을 정확하게 적용하기 위해서는 complement와 adjunct를 구분할 수 있어야 하고 구조적 관계에 대한 이해도 필요하다.

문제 풀이 과정

A박스 요약 및 핵심내용

Pronouns *one* vs *it*: *one* can replace an N' (not an N), while *it* can replace an NP.

B박스 분석 과정

▶ one은 N-bar 성분을 대체하므로 complement에 의해 수식받을 수 없다는 점을 기억해야 한다.

ⓐ one은 'poetry book'이므로 N-bar를 대체했다. 또한 modern이 adjunct이므로 one은 무조건 N-bar성분이다.

ⓑ one은'poetry book'이므로 N-bar를 대체했다. 또한 which는 speicifer이므로 one은 무조건 N-bar성분이다.

ⓒ one은 'poetry book'이므로 N-bar를 대체했다. 또한 that는 speicifer이고 'over there'이 adjunct이므로 one은 무조건 N-bar성분이다.

ⓓ one은 'book'을 의미한다. 따라서 N을 대체했으므로 잘못된 대체이다.

ⓔ one는 adjunct PP 'with a green-colored spine'에 의해 수식받으므로 N-bar성분을 대체하고 있다. 하지만 대화 맥락상 앞에 'the'가 쓰여야 한다.

풀이 과정에서 어려운 점

ⓔ one에서 N-bar성분을 대체했지만 specifier 'the'가 맥락에 의해 필요하다는 점을 놓치면 안된다.

답안

⑤

과제

〈B〉박스의 one 대체된 모든 NP들의 수형도를 그려보세요.

17. Read 〈A〉 and 〈B〉 and follow the directions. 【2.5 points】 2009-32

〈A〉

A phrase consists of a head and non-head elements. Some non-head elements complete the meaning of the head. These elements are referred to as a complement. It is a general term to denote any element whose presence is required by the head. Although the presence of a complement is normally obligatory, that of an N can be omitted. There are also elements in a phrase which describe the head rather than complete it. These elements are modifiers (or adjuncts). They can be omitted without affecting grammaticality.

〈B〉

An example of error in popular views ⓐ <u>about the mind</u> appears in the idea of a faculty of the observation. One often hears it said that we should train the observation ⓑ <u>of our students</u>; and it is imagined that by training them to observe certain things we are training them to observe anything and everything. Observation, however, relies on interest and knowledge. We have no reason to suppose that a botanist, trained in the observation ⓒ <u>of flowers</u>, will be more observant than us ⓓ <u>of the faces of the people he meets</u>. People are more likely to have their attention diverted ⓔ <u>by the objects of their special interests</u>. So training in the careful observation of the varied endings ⓕ <u>of Latin words</u>, or of the changes in chemical substances in experiment, will have no effect on the observation of pictures or the movements of the stars.

Based on 〈A〉, choose all the complement PPs from the underlined parts in 〈B〉.

① ⓐ,ⓑ,ⓒ
② ⓐ,ⓒ,ⓓ
③ ⓑ,ⓒ,ⓓ
④ ⓑ,ⓒ,ⓕ
⑤ ⓓ,ⓔ,ⓕ

출제 영역

Phrases 〉X-bar Theory 〉 Complement/Adjunct

출제 의도

Complement/Adjunct를 의미적 또는 구조적으로 구분할 수 있어야 한다.

문제 풀이 과정

A박스 요약 및 핵심내용

1. Complement

Some non-head elements complete the meaning of the head. These elements are referred to as a complement whose presence is required by the head.

2. Adjunct

elements in a phrase which describe the head rather than complete it. These elements are modifiers (or adjuncts). They can be omitted without affecting grammaticality.

B박스 분석 과정

▶ complement/adjunct 구분은 head와 의미적 관계를 잘 따져봐야 한다. 이 문제는 그런점에서 공부하기 좋은 문제이다.

ⓐ 'about the mind'는 views의 complement이다. 견해와 견해의 대상은 의미적으로 밀접하게 관련된다. 또한 view를 동사로 쓰면 the mind는 목적어로 쓰일 수 있기 때문이다.

ⓑ of our students은 observation의 목적어 의미로 쓰인것이 아니라 주어의미로 쓰였다. 즉 학생을 관찰한다는 의미가 아니라 학생이 관찰한다는 의미이다. 따라서 adjunct이다.

ⓒ of flowers는 observation의 목적어 의미로 쓰였으므로 complement이다.

ⓓ of the faces of the people he meets는 observant의 대상을 나타내므로 complement이다.

ⓔ by the objects of their special interests는 adjunct 이다. 수동화에서 by-phrase는 언제나 adjunct이다.

ⓕ of Latin words는 endings의 adjunct이다. endings의 대상이 아닌 소유의 의미(Latin words' endings)로 쓰였기 때문이다.

풀이 과정에서 어려운 점

of 전치사구가 주어나 소유의 의미로 사용될 때는 complement가 아니라는 점을 주의해야 한다.

답안

②

과제

- of-전치사구가 주어의 의미로 사용되는 경우를 정리하자.
- of-전치사구가 소유의 의미로 사용되는 경우를 정리하자.
- of-전치사구가 Head의 대상의 의미로 사용되는 경우를 정리하자.

18. Read 〈A〉 and 〈B〉 and follow the directions. 【1.5 points】 2010-36

The phrase structure rules in (1) enable English speakers to understand and produce noun phrases of any length. However, there are syntactic restrictions on the way linguistic expressions are built up by the phrase structure rules.

(1) a. NP → (D) N'
b. N' → N' PP
c. N' → N (PP)
d. PP → P NP

(2) a. *a student in London of linguistics
b. a philosopher with letters from friends
c. a student with a paper on physics
d. *a student of physics of chemistry
e. a man with books in the store

('*' indicates that the expression is ungrammatical.)

a. In (2a), both PPs are sisters to N'.
b. In (2b), both PPs are sisters to N'.
c. In (2c), both PPs are sisters to N.
d. In (2d), both PPs are sisters to N'.
e. In (2e), both PPs are sisters to N'.

Choose all the statements in 〈B〉 that correctly describe the structural relations of PPs within the noun phrases in 〈A〉.

① a, b
② a, b, e
③ a, d
④ b, e
⑤ c, d, e

출제 영역

Phrases > X-bar Theory

출제 의도

Complement와 Adjunct의 구분할 수 있어야 하고 구조적 차이점도 기술할 수 있어야 한다.

문제 풀이 과정

A박스 요약 및 핵심내용

1. Complement와 Adjunct의 구분과 구조적 차이점:

(1) a. NP → (D) N' (Specifier rule)
b. N' → N' PP (Adjunct rule)
c. N' → N (PP) (Complement rule)
d. PP → P NP (PP rule)

(1)의 PS-rule에 따른 구조

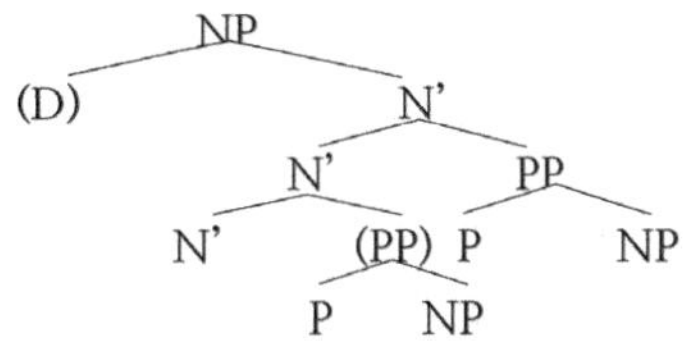

2. Complement와 Adjunct의 ordering:

(2) a. *a student in London of linguistics
b. a philosopher with letters from friends
c. a student with a paper on physics
d. *a student of physics of chemistry
e. a man with books in the store

▶ (a)는 complement가 adjunct보다 선행해야하는 점을 말하고, (d)는 complement는 반복될 수 없다는 점을 언급한다.

B박스 분석 과정

a. In (2a), both PPs are sisters to N'.
▶ 'in London'-adjunct (N'의 sister), 'of linguistics'-complement (N의 sister)
b. In (2b), both PPs are sisters to N'.
▶ 'with letters'-adjunct (N'의 sister), 'from friends'-adjunct (N'의 sister)
c. In (2c), both PPs are sisters to N.
▶ 'with a paper'-adjunct (N'의 sister), 'on physics'-paper의 complement (N의 sister)
d. In (2d), both PPs are sisters to N'.
▶ 'of physics'-complement (N의 sister), 'of chemistry'-complement (N의 sister)
e. In (2e), both PPs are sisters to N'.
▶ 'with books'-adjunct (N'의 sister), 'in the store'-adjunct (N'의 sister)

풀이 과정에서 어려운 점

Complement와 adjunct의 구조적 차이점을 파악해야 한다.

답안

④

과제

지문의 (2)비문 (a)와 (d)가 (1)의 구구조 규칙에 근거해 어떻게 위반되는지 설명해 보자.

19. Read the passage in 〈A〉 and the sentences in 〈B〉, and follow the directions. 【5 points】

2016-B06

A PP modifier has distinct grammatical functions; it can be either a Complement exemplified by the underlined PP in (1a) or an Adjunct as in (1b).

(1) a. the specialist in phonology
    b. the specialist at the stage

Two types of syntactic arguments can be presented for the structural distinction between PP Complements and PP Adjuncts. First, they are strictly ordered when they both occur as postnominal modifiers, as the contrast in (2) shows.

(2) a. The specialist in phonology at the stage
    b. *The specialist at the stage in phonology

Another syntactic argument can be formulated in relation to Wh-movement as shown in (3): NPs within PP Complements can be preposed, while NPs within PP Adjuncts cannot.

(3) a. What area of linguistics is he a specialist in?
    b. *Which place is he a specialist at?

Note: * indicates that the sentence is ungrammatical

a. He is a contender with a knee injury.
b. He is a contender for the PGA title.

Based on the description in 〈A〉, identify the grammatical function of the underlined PPs in 〈B〉. Then provide two pairs of evidence for your identification, using BOTH sentences in 〈B〉: a pair of NPs and a pair of wh-questions, with ungrammaticality marked with an asterisk (*) at the beginning of the evidence.

출제 영역

Phrases > X-bar Theory

출제 의도

Complement와 Adjunct를 구분할 수 있어야 하고, 이들의 어순관계나 wh-이동 제약관계를 설명할 수 있어야 한다.

문제 풀이 과정

A박스 요약 및 핵심내용

1. Complement vs Adjunct 구분:

(1) a. the specialist <u>in phonology</u>
b. the specialist <u>at the stage</u>

2. Complement vs Adjunct 어순:

(2) a. The specialist in phonology at the stage
b. *The specialist at the stage in phonology

3. Wh-movement 이동 제약
NPs within PP Complements can be preposed, while NPs within PP Adjuncts cannot.

(3) a. What area of linguistics is he a specialist in?
b. *Which place is he a specialist at?

B박스 분석 과정

▶ contender '도전자'의 도전의 대상인 'for the PGA title'이 complement이고, 'with a knee injury'처럼 부상 여부는 '도전자'와 의미적 관련성이 없으므로 adjunct이다. complement vs adjunct 구분이 됐다면 어순관계나 wh-이동 가능여부를 판단할 수 있다.

a. He is a contender <u>with a knee injury</u>.
b. He is a contender <u>for the PGA title</u>.

풀이 과정에서 어려운 점

핵어 'contender'의 의미를 알아야 complement/adjunct를 정확하게 판단할 수 있다. 그러나 단어가 좀 어렵다.

답안

The underlined PP in (a) is an adjunct, and the PP in (b) is a complement as follows: '*He is a contender with a knee injury for the PGA title'. 'He is a contender for the PGA title with a knee injury'. '*What kind of injury is he a contender with?'. 'What kind of title is he a contender for?.'

과제

〈B〉문장들에서 NP들의 수형도를 그려보자.

20. Read the passage and follow the directions. 【2 points】 2020-B01

There is an intriguing phenomenon in English in which two semantically related constituents are separated, as shown below.

(1) a. All the students will work hard.
b. The students will all work hard.

In both (1a) and (1b), the quantifier *all* modifies the subject *the students.* What is interesting is that in sentence (1b), the quantifier positioned after the subject forms a discontinuous constituent with no major change in meaning.

This fact can be straightforwardly accounted for if it is assumed that the entire constituent *all the students* is base-generated in the _______ position of VP. As illustrated in (2a), *all the students* undergoes movement to the surface subject position. By contrast, in (2b), just part of the constituent, *the students,* moves to the subject position, leaving *all* behind in its base position, marked as [*all* t_i].

(2) a. [$_{TP}$ [all the students]$_i$ will [VP t_i work hard]]
b.

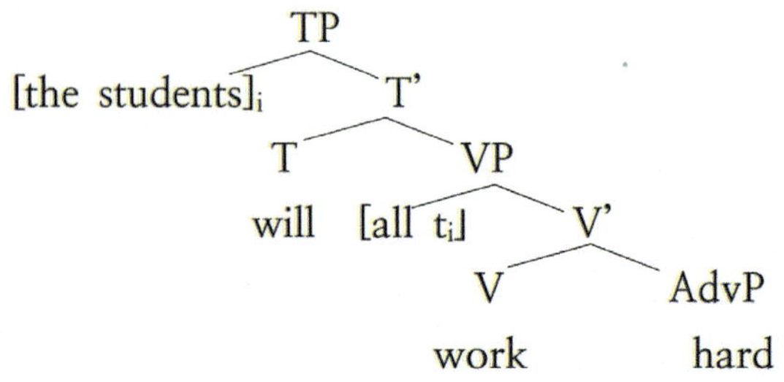

This account is based upon 'VP-internal subject hypothesis,' which states that a subject is base-generated in the ______ position of VP and in turn moves to the ______ position of Tense Phrase (TP).

Fill in the three blanks with the ONE most appropriate word. Use the SAME word for all the blanks.

출제 영역

Phrases > X-bar Theory

출제 의도

'All'의 floating현상을 VP-internal subject hypothesis와 이동현상을 통해 이해하고 설명할 수 있어야 한다.

문제 풀이 과정

1. 'All' floating:
the quantifier positioned after the subject forms a discontinuous constituent with no major change in meaning:

(1) a. *All* the students will work hard.
    b. The students will *all* work hard.

2. 'all'의 position
In (2a), *all the students* undergoes movement to the surface subject position. By contrast, in (2b), just part of the constituent, *the students*, moves to the subject position, leaving *all* behind in its base position, marked as [*all* t_i].

3. VP-internal subject hypothesis
A subject is base-generated in the specifier position of VP and in turn moves to the specifier position of Tense Phrase (TP).

풀이 과정에서 어려운 점

VP-internal subject hypothesis 개념이 종종 문제에서 언급된다. 잘 이해해야 한다.

답안

specifier

과제

카니 'Syntax'교재에서 DP-이동을 어떻게 설명하는지 살펴보세요. (카니책은 VP-internal subject hypothesis를 가정하고 있습니다.)

21. Read the passage and follow the direction. 【2 points】 2021-A03

In the languages of the world, we have two different types of adposition: a preposition type (e.g., English) and a postposition type (e.g., Korean). With the preposition type, we find that a preposition head precedes its complement as in (1a). As for the postposition type, a postposition follows its complement as in (1b).

(1) a. Preposition

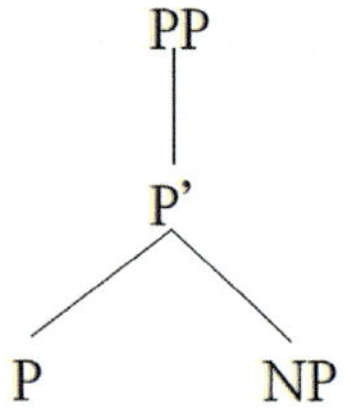

b. Postposition

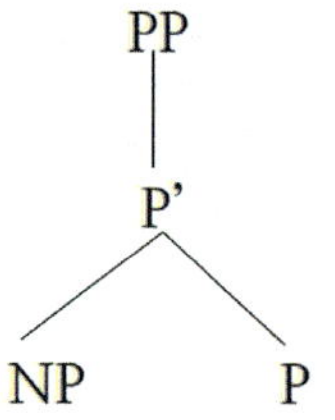

However, some linguistics argue that all languages uniformly have the preposition system and the seemingly postposition system is derived from the preposition type by movement as in (2).

(2)

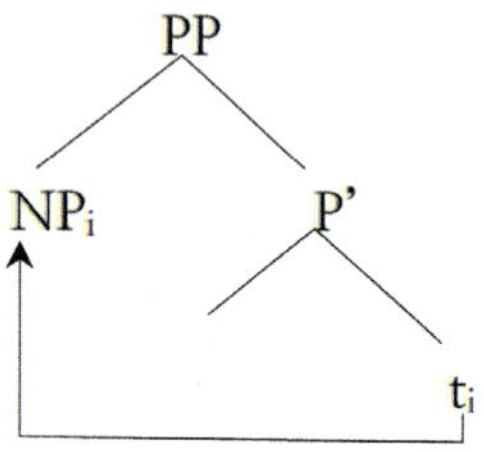

We can apply the analysis in (2) to the so-called particle structure.

(3) They left $[_{PP}\ [_{NP}$ this part$]_i$ out $t_i]$.

In (3), NP *this part* moves from the ________ position of the head *out* to the specifier position.

Fill in the blank with the ONE most appropriate word from the passage.

출제 영역

Phrases 〉X-bar Theory

출제 의도

전치사가 NP 뒤에 위치하는 Postpostion type과 phrasal verb에서 동사와 전치사(particle)의 분리 현상을 하나의 동일한 구조에서 기인한다는 점을 이해해야 한다.

문제 풀이 과정

1. Two different types of adposition: a preposition type and a postposition type
2. Uniformity : the seemingly postposition system is derived from the preposition type in (2)
3. Particle structure

NP *this part* moves from the complement position of the head *out* to the specifier position.

(3) They left [$_{PP}$ [$_{NP}$ this part]$_i$ out t_i].

풀이 과정에서 어려운 점

한국어의 postposition의 개념은 낯설다. 하지만 어려운 개념은 아니다.

답안

complement

과제

(3)과 같이 phrasal verb에서 동사와 전치사의 분리현상을 NP의 이동으로 설명하지만, '트포'에서는 다른 방식으로 설명한다. NP-movement 부분을 읽고 정리해 보자.

22. Read the Passage and follow the directions. 【4 points】 2021-B05

To account for some syntactic phenomena in English, we can resort to phrasal categories such as VP, TP, CP. and so on. First, let us assume that only constituents which belong to the same phrasal category can be coordinated. For example, NP can conjoin with another NP, but not with AP.

(1) a. The student or the teacher
    b. *The student or very pretty

The same restriction also holds true with clausal structures. The bracketed structures in (2a) and (2b) are clearly different, since they cannot be coordinated by the conjunction *or*, as shown in (2c).

(2) a. We didn't intend [you to hurt him].
    b. We didn't intend [for him to hurt you].
    c. *We didn't intend [you to hurt him] or [for him to hurt you].

So, based on the phrasal category and the assumption about coordination, we can explain the ungrammaticality of the sentences such as (2c).

Second, the restriction on wh-cleft sentences can also be attributed to phrasal categories.

(3) What I'll do is [$_{VP}$ postpone the meeting].

VP can be in the focus position (the position after *be* verb) of wh-cleft sentences like (3). Consider further the following examples.

(4) a. Bill promised [$_{CP}$ ∅ PRO to behave himself].
    b. What Bill promised was [$_{CP}$ ∅ PRO to behave himself].

(5) a. They believe [$_{TP}$ him to be innocent].
    b. *What they believe is [$_{TP}$ him to be innocent].

The verb *promise* in (4a) is known to take a CP (Complementizer Phrase) complement which is headed by a null complementizer ∅, and we find that CP can be in the focus position, as shown in (4b). Meanwhile, in (5a), the verb *believe* requires a TP (Tense Phrase) complement, and from the ungrammaticality of (5b), it is clear that TP cannot be in the focus position of a wh-ceft sentence. Thus, bsed on the types ofphrasal categories, we can explain the restriction on wh-cleft sentences.

Note 1: * indicates ungrammaticality of the sentence.
Note 2: 'PRO' is a null pronoun which represents the understood subject of some infinitive clauses.

(i) She argued persuasively or that their offer should be rejected.
(ii) They offered us a choice of red wine, white wine, or beer.
(iii) What he claims is that he was insulted.
(iv) What we hadn't intended was you to get hurt.

Based on ⟨A⟩, choose ONE ungrammatical sentence between (i) and (ii) in ⟨B⟩ and ONE grammatical sentence between (iii) and (iv) in ⟨B⟩. Then, explain why the chosen sentences are ungrammatical or grammatical on the basis of the description in ⟨A⟩.

출제 영역

Phrases > Clause (CP vs TP)

출제 의도

범주가 문법성 설명에 매우 중요한 역할을 한다. 특히 coordination과 wh-cleft sentence의 focus position에서 중요한 역할을 한다는 점을 설명할 수 있어야 한다.

출제 의도

A박스 요약 및 핵심내용

1. Syntactic phenomena의 phrasal categories 의존성:
 a. NP can conjoin with another NP, but not with AP.

 (1) a. The student or the teacher
  b. *The student or very pretty

 b. The same restriction also holds true with clausal structures.

 (2) c. *We didn't intend [you to hurt him] or [for him to hurt you].

2. wh-cleft sentences와 phrasal categories
 a. VP can be in the focus position
 (3) What I'll do is [$_{VP}$ postpone the meeting].

 b. CP can be in the focus position
 (4) b. What Bill promised was [$_{CP}$ ∅ PRO to behave himself].
 (5) b. *What they believe is [$_{TP}$ him to be innocent].

▶ (4a)와 (5a)는 Control과 ECM구문의 차이를 보여주고 있다.

B박스 분석 과정

(i) She argued persuasively or that their offer should be rejected.
(ii) They offered us a choice of red wine, white wine, or beer.
▶ (i)에서 AdvP 'persuasively'와 CP 'that 절'을 연결해서 비문이다. (ii)에서 NP들을 연결했으므로 정문이다.
(iii) What he claims is that he was insulted.
(iv) What we hadn't intended was you to get hurt.
▶ (iii)에서 focus position에 CP 'that he was insulted'이므로 정문이지만, (iv)에서 'you to get hurt'는 TP이므로 비문이다. 이 clause가 TP 라는 것은 main verb 'intended'가 ECM 동사라는 것을 통해 알 수 있다.

풀이 과정에서 어려운 점

(i)에서 'or'가 무엇을 연결하고 있는지 잘 파악해야 하고, (iv)에서 'you to get hurt'가 TP라는 것을 동사 intended를 보고 알아야 한다. intended는 TP를 complement로 취하는 ECM동사이기 때문이다.

답안

The sentence (i) is ungrammatical, since the AdvP, 'persuasively' and CP, 'that their offer should be rejected' cannot be coordinated by the conjunction 'or'. The sentence (iii) is grammatical, since CP, 'that he was insulted' can be in the focus position.

과제

ECM와 Control구문의 차이점을 카니 'Syntax' 원서를 참고하여 정리하세요.

23. Read the passage and follow the directions. 【4 points】 2018-A12

It is well known that coordinate conjunctions can conjoin constituents of the same grammatical category but cannot conjoin constituents of different grammatical categories, as exemplified in (1) and (2).

(1) a. fond of a dog and afraid of a tiger
b. very slowly and very steadily
c. a princess of Denmark and a prince of the United Kingdom
d. I think that Mary likes poems and Susan novels.
e. I think that Mary likes poems and that Susan likes novels

(2) a. *like a dog and afraid of a tiger
b. *slowly and the car
c. *a princess of Denmark and with long hair
d. *I believe Mary to be honest and that Susan is kind.
e. *I believe that Mary is honest and Susan to be kind.

AP can conjoin with another AP, AdvP with another AdvP. NP or DP with another NP or DP, TP with another TP, and CP with another CP.

TP, meaning Tense Phrase, is a clause that does not include a complementizer like Mary likes poems in (3a). CP, meaning Complementizer Phrase, is a clause that includes a complementizer. The embedded clause of sentence (3a) has the structure in (3b).

(3) a. I think that Mary likes poems.
b.

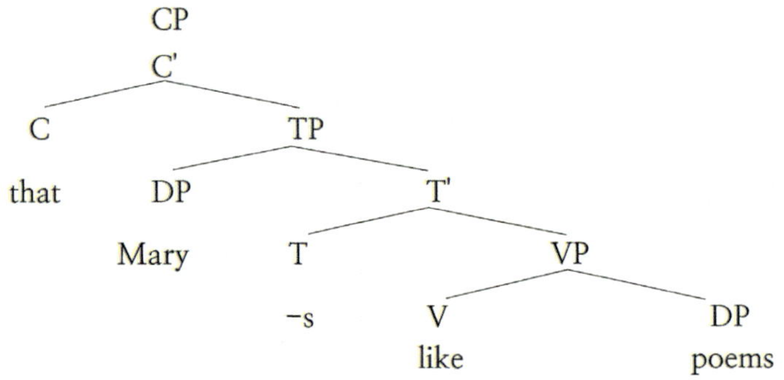

Note: * indicates the ungrammaticality of the sentence.

State whether sentence (4) and sentence (5) can be conjoined with the coordinate conjunction but as in sentence (6). Then, explain why, identifying the grammatical category of sentence (4) and that of sentence (5).

(4) I am feeling thirsty.
(5) Should I save my last cola till later?
(6) I am feeling thirsty but should I save my last cola till later?

출제 영역

Phrases > Clause (CP vs TP)

출제 의도

Clause의 범주를 구분할 수 있어야 한다. ordinary clause는 CP이고, Exceptional clause는 TP이다. 비록 complementizer가 외현적으로 실현되지 않더라도 null complementizer가 존재하므로 CP가 된다.

문제 풀이 과정

A박스 요약 및 핵심내용

1. coordination 조건

   It can conjoin constituents of the same grammatical category

2. TP와 CP의 구분

   TP is a clause that does not include a complementizer. CP is a clause that includes a complementizer.

B박스 분석 과정

(4)는 complementizer가 없지만 null complementizer의 존재로 인해 CP

(5)는 'should'의 inversion시 complementizer자리로 이동하므로 CP

(6) CP와 CP의 conjoin이므로 정문판단

풀이 과정에서 어려운 점

〈A〉박스에서 null complenentizer와 inversion시 AUX의 이동위치에 대한 정보를 제공하지 않는다. → 배경지식을 추가로 요구하는 문제

답안

The sentence (4) and (5) can be conjoin with the coordinate conjunction. (4) is a CP that has a null complementizer, and (5) is also a CP that has an inverted auxiliary in the complementizer position.

과제

TP와 CP 구분을 정확히 할 수 있어야 한다. 나는 이 구분을 어떻게 하고 있는지 말해보자.

24. Read the passages and follow the directions. 2007-전국-16변형

> Consider the sentences:
>
> (1) Max believed that there was a rose in the garden.
> (2) Max believed Mary to have chocolate.
>
> (1) and (2) show that the verb *believe* can take as its complement a finite clause, in which the verb contains the information of tense and or ________, or a non-finite clause, in which the verb does not. Consider further the following sentences:
>
> (3) Max told Mary that there was a rose in the garden.
> (4) Max told Mary to have chocolate.
>
> The verb *tell* can take two complements, as in (3), where the NP *Mary* functions as the object of the main clause. Given (2) and (4), it appears that the verbs *believe* and *tell* behave alike. But, a sharp contrast arises between (5) and (6) when the NP is replaced by the expletive *there.*
>
> (5) Max believed there to be a rose in the garden.
> (6) *Max told there to be a rose in the garden.
>
> Traditionally, the ungrammaticality of (6) is due to the constraint on the type of object that the verb *tell* takes, as shown in (4) and (7).
>
> (4) Max told Mary to have chocolate.
> (7) *Max told the tree to have chocolate.
>
> Another way of accounting for the difference in (5) and (6) is to rely on the distribution of the expletives. The sentences in (8) and (9) indicate that expletives always occupy the subject position.
>
> (8) a. There is a rose in the garden, isn't there?
> b. It is raining, isn't it?
> (9) a. *I talked about there. (expletive *there*)
> b. *I saw it. (expletive *it*)
>
> *Note*: * indicates ungrammaticality of the expression.

The sentences (6) and (7) are ungrammatical as shown above. Explain why the two sentence are ungrammatical.

출제 영역

Phrases 〉 Clauses 〉 Exceptional vs Control

출제 의도

ECM과 Control 구문을 구분하는 문제이다. believe 동사 바로 뒤 NP는 내포절의 주어이고 tell동사 뒤 NP는 동사의 목적어이다. 따라서 tell 뒤의 NP는 동사의 논항이므로 동사와 의미적 제약(선택제약)을 유지해야 한다. 이 차이점을 이해한다면 동사 뒤 허사 there의 분포에 대해 설명할 수 있다.

문제 풀이 과정

(5)의 believe 뒤 NP자리는 내포절의 주어자리이다. 따라서 허사 there가 believed 뒤에 위치할 수 있다. 하지만 (6)의 tell 뒤 NP자리는 동사의 목적어자리이다. 그래서 허사 there가 그 자리에 위치할 수 없다.

(5) Max believed there to be a rose in the garden.
(6) *Max told there to be a rose in the garden.

동사 'tell' 뒤의 NP는 동사의 목적이므로 동사의 논항이다. 따라서 동사 tell은 바로 뒤 명사자리에 말하는 것을 들을 수 있는 개체만 허용된다.

(4) Max told Mary to have chocolate.
(7) *Max told the tree to have chocolate.

풀이 과정에서 어려운 점

Main verb의 논항구조를 정확하게 알아야 한다.

답안

agreement
The following position of the main verb 'tell' is an object position of the verb, not a subject position of the embedded clause. Expletive 'there' cannot occur in the position since it always occupies a subject position. The verb 'tell' imposes a semantic constraint on its object, and thus the inanimate entity 'the tree' cannot be used as the object of the verb.

과제

a. Exceptional clause 특징을 정리하세요.
b. ECM동사를 모두 적으세요.

CHAPTER

03

Binding Theory

영역	출제년도	내용
1. C-command	2020-A06	NPI
2. Anaphors	2017-B06 2013-35 2015-A10 2018-B06	two or three branching? BC and LC Smallest clause (영역) Binding and movement
3. Pronouns		
4. Referential Expressions		

❑ 연도별 출제빈도

2002	2003	2004	2005	2006	2007	2008	2009	2010	2011	2012	2013	2014	2015	2016	2017	2018	2019	2020	2021	2022	2023	2024	2025	2026
											*		*		*	*		*						?

1. Read the passage and follow the directions. 【4 points】 2020-A06

There is a class of words, such as *yet* and *any*, called 'Negative Polarity Item (NPIs).' They are allowed in sentences containing a negative word such as *not*, as illustrated below.

(1) a. The defense strategy had not been determined yet.
 b. *The defense strategy had been determined yet.

However, there is an additional structural condition for an NPI to be licensed by the negation *not*. As shown in (2), the negation has to c-command the NPI.

(2) *Any defense strategy had not been determined.

(3) A node c-commands its sister nodes and all the daughter nodes of its sister nodes.

In (2), given the definition of c-command in (3), *not* does not c-command *any*. Hence, the sentence is ungrammatical.

Temporal and locational adverbials can be structurally ambiguous in that they can modify either a matrix element or an embedded element. In (4a) below, *yesterday* can modify the embedded *knew the answer*, as illustrated in (4b). Let us refer to this reading as 'embedded reading.' In the embedded reading, it is asked whether Mark Knew the answer yesterday. By contrast, *yesterday* an also modify the matrix predicate *wondered*, as shown in (4c). Let us refer to this reading as 'matrix reading.' In the matrix reading, yesterday is when Celin wondered about Mark.

(4) a. Celin wondered if Mark knew the answer yesterday.
 b. [Celin wondered [if Mark knew the answer yesterday]]: embedded reading
 c. [Celin wondered [if Mark knew the answer] yesterday]: matrix reading

(i) Mary said that Justin did not sing in any room.
(ii) Mary did not say that Justin sang in any room.

For the sentences in 〈B〉, identify whether each sentence has a matrix reading, embedded reading, or both. Then, explain your answer on the basis of the description in 〈A〉.

출제 영역

C-command & NPI

출제 의도

NPIs가 부정어에 의해 c-command되어야 한다는 조건을 이해해야하고, 이 조건을 부사어구의 수식관계와 연계시켰다. 부사어구가 주절의 동사를 수식할 수 있고, 내포절의 동사를 수식할 수 있다. 부사어구에 NPI가 포함된다면 수식관계는 한정될 수 있다는 점을 파악해야 한다. 구조적인 측면을 대략적으로 이미지화 할 수 있다면 도움이된다.

문제 풀이 과정

A박스 요약 및 핵심내용

1. NPIs의 분포:

An NPI should be licensed by the negation 'not', and the negation has to c-command the NPI.

2. Temporal and locational adverbials의 수식관계에 따른 해석

a. Celin wondered if Mark knew the answer yesterday.

b. [Celin wondered [if Mark knew the answer yesterday]]: embedded reading

c. [Celin wondered [if Mark knew the answer] yesterday]: matrix reading

B박스 분석 과정

(ⅰ) Mary said that Justin did not sing in any room.

'any'는 not에 의해 c-command 되어야하므로 내포절의 동사 sing만을 수식한다. → 'embedded reading'

(만약 'in any room'의 said를 수식한다면 any는 not에 의해 c-command되지 않는다.)

(ⅱ) Mary did not say that Justin sang in any room.

'not'상위절에 위치하므로 in any room이 어디를 수식하든지 not에 의해 c-command된다. → 'matrix reading' and 'embedded reading'

풀이 과정에서 어려운 점

'in any room'에서 any가 not에 의해 c-command될 수 있는지 구조적으로 이해할 수 있어야 한다.

답안

The sentence (ⅰ) has an embedded reading, since the negation 'not' that is in the embedded clause c-commands the NPI 'any', which means that 'in any room' modifies the embedded predicate. The sentence (ⅱ) has both readings since the negation can c-command the NPI 'any' regardless of its position, which means that the adverbial can modify both matrix and embedded predicates.

과제

1. 아래 두 문장들의 수형도를 그려보자. 중의성이 있는 문장은 각 의미에 따라 각 수형도를 그려보자.

a. Mary said that Justin did not sing in any room.

b. Mary did not say that Justin sang in any room.

2. NPIs와 PPIs(Positive Polarity Items)를 아는 대로 적어보자.

2. Read the passage in 〈A〉 and the sentences in 〈B〉, and follow the directions. 【5 points】

2017-B06

Anaphors such as *each other* have to be bound by their antecedent. An anaphor must satisfy two condition to be bound. An anaphor can be bound if it is coindexed (i.e., coreferential) with its antecedent and is also c-commanded by that antecedent within the smallest clause or noun phrase containing the anaphor. A node c-command its sister and all the decedents of its sister. For example, in (1), B c-commands C, D, E, F, G, H, I, J, and K; however, I c-commands only H, which it its sister. It does not c-command any other nodes.

(1)

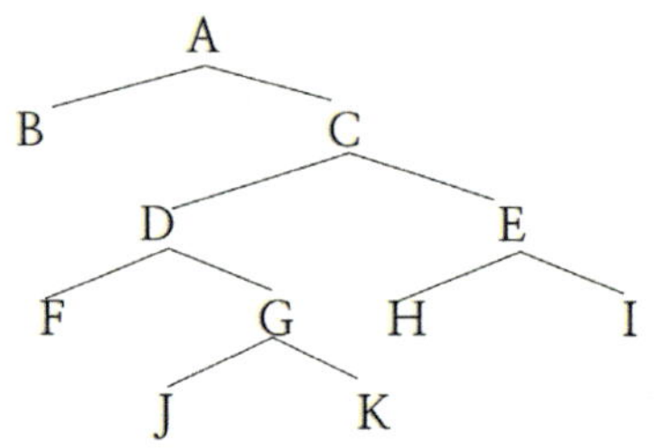

Consider the two structures for the verb phrase in the double object construction (2). (3) is a ternary (three) branching structure, which is a kind of multiple branching structure, and (4) a binary branching structure.

(2) Tom will give Mary a book.

(3)

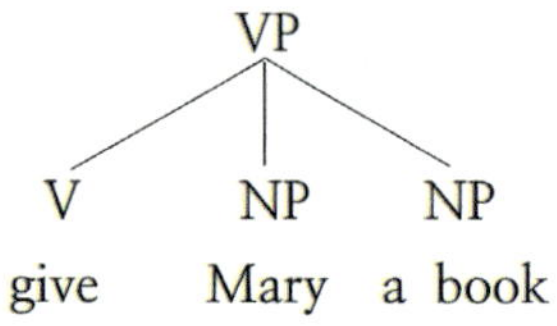

(4)

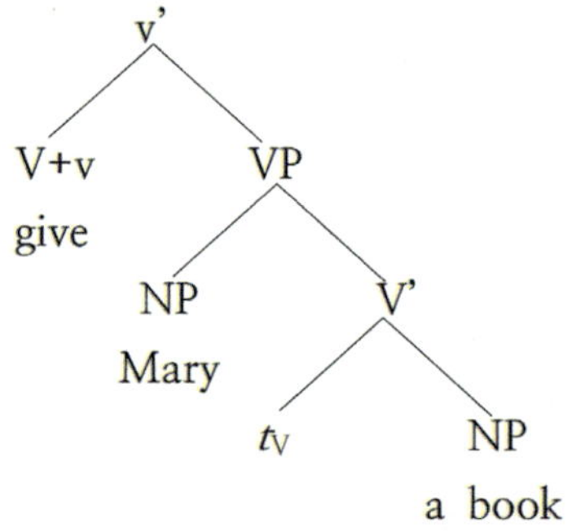

In (3) and (4), the direct and indirect objects have different structure relations.

(i) Mary showed the boys$_i$ each other$_i$.
(ii) *Mary showed each other$_i$ the boys$_i$.
(In the examples the boys and each other refer to the same people.)

Note: * indicates that the sentence is ungrammatical.

Identify which VP structure, (3) or (4), can account for the ungrammaticality of sentence (ii) in 〈B〉. Then, explain why one, but not other structure, can account for the ungrammaticality by using the c-command relation described in 〈A〉.

출제 영역

Bindding Theory & C-command

출제 의도

결속이론에서 c-command는 매우 중요한 개념이다. 선행사가 anaphor를 c-command하는 구조가 조건이 된다. 이러한 구조적 조건이 충족되기 위해 ternary branching 구조와 binary branching구조 중 어느 구조가 적절한지 판단할 수 있어야 한다.

문제 풀이 과정

A박스 요약 및 핵심내용

1. anaphor의 결속조건 : An anaphor can be bound if it is coindexed (i.e., coreferential) with its antecedent and is also c-commanded by that antecedent within the smallest clause or noun phrase containing the anaphor.
2. c-command
3. VP 구조 : ternary branching (트포) vs. binary branching (double object construction)

B박스 분석 과정

(i) Mary showed the boys$_i$ each other$_i$.
(ii) *Mary showed each other$_i$ the boys$_i$.

3분지 구조 분석이 맞다면 문장 (ii)도 정문이어야 한다. 선행사 'the boys'가 anaphor 'each other'를 c-command하고 서로 co-index되기 때문이다. 하지만 (ii)가 비문이므로 the boys가 each other를 c-command할 수 없는 이분지 구조가 적절하다.

풀이 과정에서 어려운 점

give나 show같은 두 개의 complement를 취하는 동사(double object construction)를 binary branching 구조로 표현하려면 VP-shell 구조로 나타내야 한다. 이 VP-shell구조는 임용에서 매우 심화된 개념이라서 어렵게 느껴질 수 있다.

답안

The structure (4) can account for the ungrammaticality of sentence (ii). The ternary structure (3) allows the two NPs to c-command mutually, which cannot account for the ungrammaticality of (ii). The binary branching structure in (4) that does not allow the second NP to c-command the anaphor as in (ii), which can account for the ungrammaticality of (ii).

과제

'이동걸영어학' 유튜브 채널(https://youtu.be/CWg7PpRcGoQ?si=cOMvusbku9h3L8IC) 에서 시청하고 내용 정리하기

3. Read ⟨A⟩ and ⟨B⟩ and answer the question. 【2 points】 2013-35

A reflexive (e.g., himself) or a reciprocal (e.g., each other) in general meets both of the two constraints below.

The Binding Constraint (BC)
A reflexive or a reciprocal (Y) must be bound by its antecedent (X).
[X binds Y if and only if X c-commands Y and X and Y are co-indexed (thereby co-referring); a constituent X c-commands its sister constituent Y and any constituent Z that is contained within Y.]

The c-command relation is represented in the tree diagram below.

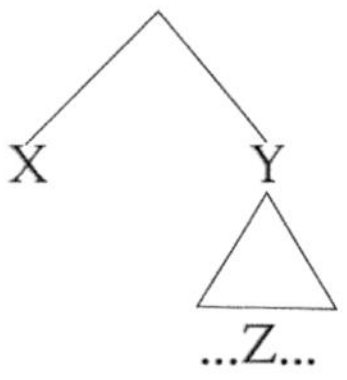

The Locality Constraint (LC)
A reflexive or a reciprocal must find its antecedent within the local binding domain.
[The local binding domain is the smallest clause containing a reflexive or a reciprocal.]

For example, in (1), the reflexive violates the BC, and in (2), it violates the LC.

(1) *Mary hopes Hichael$_i$'s father represents himself$_i$.
(2) *John$_i$ thinks Mary should marry himself$_i$.

Cases	Types of constraints violated
a. *Mary expects each other$_i$'s mothers will dance with the two boys$_i$.	LC only
b. *Their$_i$ teacher thinks Bill hit each other$_i$'s friends.	both BC and LC
c. *Each other$_i$ persuaded their$_i$ sons to leave.	BC only
d. *John wanted the girls$_i$ to know that he would help with each other$_i$'s homework.	both BC and LC

Which of the following lists all and only the cases in ⟨B⟩ that correctly illustrate the violation(s) of the constraint(s) described in ⟨A⟩?

① a, b ② a, c ③ b, c ④ b, d ⑤ c, d

출제 영역

Binding Theory

출제 의도

대용어의 결속 조건은 결속과 결속 영역의 개념으로 이루어진다. 결속 조건으로 비문을 설명할 때 각 개념의 어느 부분이 문제가 되는지 정확하게 파악할 수 있어야 한다.

문제 풀이 과정

A박스 요약 및 핵심내용

결속 조건은 크게 두 개념으로 구성된다. 하나는 결속, 다른 하나는 결속 영역이다. 이 두 개념을 소개한다.

1. The Binding Constraint (BC) : A reflexive or a reciprocal (Y) must be bound(co-index and c-command) by its antecedent (X).
2. The Locality Constraint (LC) : A reflexive or a reciprocal must find its antecedent within the local binding domain (the smallest clause containing a reflexive or a reciprocal).

B박스 분석 과정

결속영역은 '[ ]'로 표시함

a. *Mary expects [each other$_i$'s mothers will dance with the two boys$_i$.]

▶ 선행사와 anaphor가 결속영역에 있지만 each other가 the two boys를 결속(not c-command)하지 않는다.

b. *Their$_i$ teacher thinks [Bill hit each other$_i$'s friends.]

▶ 선행사가 결속영역 밖에 위치하고 each other를 c-command하지 않으므로 결속하지 않는다.

c. *[Each other$_i$ persuaded their$_i$ sons to leave.]

▶ 선행사와 each other가 같은 결속영역에 위치하지만 선행사가 each other를 c-command할 수 없으므로 결속할 수 없다.

d. *John wanted the girls$_i$ to know [that he would help with each other$_i$'s homework].

▶ 선행사 the girls와 each other를 결속하지만 결속영역 밖에 위치하므로 비문이다.

풀이 과정에서 어려운 점

결속이론으로 문법성을 설명하는데 결속과 영역의 개념을 구분해서 설명하는 방식이 다소 어렵게 느껴질 수 있다. (익숙한 이론을 살짝만 바꿔도 어렵게 느껴지고 혼동될 수 있다. 항상 주의해야 한다.)

답안

③

과제

〈B〉박스의 문장들을 수형도로 그려보자.

4. Read the passage and fill in the blank with ONE word. 【2 points】 2015-A10

The sentences in (1) show three types of NPs: the reflexive pronoun, the ordinary pronoun, and the proper noun.

(1) a. John likes himself.
    b. Mary met him.
    c. John came.

The reflexive pronoun should have the antecedent in the sentence from which it picks up its reference as shown in (2), with the coindexed NPs indicating the same referent. This sharply contrasts with the ordinary pronoun and the proper noun in (3).

(2) a. $John_i$ introduced $himself_i$ to Mary.
    b. *Himself came.

(3) a. $John_i$ introduced him_j to Mary.
    b. John introduced Bill to Mary.

The existence of the antecedent in the sentence, however, is not a sufficient condition to license the reflexive pronoun, as shown in (4).

(4) a. *$John_i$ thinks that $himself_i$ is intelligent.
    b. John tole $Mary_i$ about $herself_i$.

The examples in (2) and (4) show that the reflexive pronoun finds its antecedent in the smallest ________ that contains it. The sentences in (2b) and (4a) are thus ungrammatical in contrast to those in (2a) and (4b).

출제 영역

Binding Theory

출제 의도

대용어(anaphor)의 결속조건 영역의 개념을 빈칸으로 묻고 있다. 결속 조건은 결속의 개념과 결속 영역의 개념이 매우 중요하다.

문제 풀이 과정

1. NP의 세 가지 유형 소개 : reflexive, pronoun, R-expression
2. Reflexive의 결속 조건 : '..the reflexive pronoun finds its antecedent in the smallest ________ that contains it.'
3. 빈칸은 결속 영역에 대해 묻고 있다.

풀이 과정에서 어려운 점

평이함

답안

Clause

과제

NP의 세 가지 유형(Anaphor, Pronoun, and R-expression) 에 대한 결속 조건을 암기하지

5. Read the passages and follow the directions. 【4 points】 2018-B06

Sentences must satisfy various principles to be grammatically correct. Consider the following sentence.

(1) a. It seems that Tom admires Mary.
  b. *Tom seems that he admires Mary.

Sentence (1a) is grammatical but sentence (1b) is ungrammatical since the matrix subject *Tom* has no theta role.

Next, consider sentences containing an anaphor.

(2) a. Tom thinks that $Mary_i$ admires $herself_i$.
  b. *Tom_i thinks that Mary admires $himself_i$.

(3) a. Tom expects $Mary_i$ to admire $herself_i$.
  b. *Tom_i expects Mary to admire $himself_i$.

Sentences (2a) and (3a) are grammatical since the reflexive pronoun *herself* is in the same clause as, and bound by, the antecedent *Mary*. However, sentences (2b) and (3b) are ungrammatical since the reflexive pronoun *himself* does not occur in the same clause as the antecedent *Tom*, violating the binding condition, which requires a reflexive pronoun to be bound by its antecedent in its binding domain, which is the smallest clause containing the anaphor.

Finally, consider the following sentences.

(4) a. It seems that Tom is believed to admire Mary.
  b. *Tom seems that it is believed to admire Mary.

Sentence (4a) is grammatically correct since no violation of grammatical principles has occurred. However, sentence (4b) is ungrammatical since the movement of the matrix subject has violated a constrain which bans a subject from crossing another subject.

Consider the following sentence.

(5) Tom_i appears to Mary to be believed by his friends to brag about $himself_i$.

In the above sentence, the reflexive pronoun *himself* is in the lowest embedded clause, whereas its antecedent *Tom* is in the subject position of the matrix clause.

State whether sentence (5) in 〈B〉 is syntactically well-formed or ill-formed. Then, explain why, discussing whether the matrix subject can be assigned a theta role, whether it violates any movement constraint, and whether the anaphor can be bound.

출제 영역

NP-movement & Binding Theory

출제 의도

NP-movement가 적용되는 과정을 묻는다. 결속이론과 의미역할당 개념이 결합되었지만 NP이동 과정을 정확하게 이해한다면 다른 연계 개념은 어렵지 않다. NP가 생성된 위치를 알아야 하고 그 곳에서 NP이동 제약 ('a constraint which bans a subject from crossing another subject')을 위반하지 않고 최종 목적지인 주절의 주어자리로 이동하는 과정을 말할 수 있어야 한다. 이 과정에서 reflexive의 결속 조건을 준수하는지까지 언급해야 한다.

문제 풀이 과정

A박스 요약 및 핵심내용

〈A〉에서 세가지를 언급한다. 첫째, seem류 동사의 논항구조이다. 즉, raising predicate를 언급한다. 내포절의 주어가 주절의 주어자리로 이동해야 한다. 둘째, reflexive는 동일절의 선행사와 결속해야 한다는 결속조건을 언급한다. 통사론에서 매우 중요하고 기본적인 개념이므로 꼭 숙지해야 한다. 마지막으로 NP-이동의 제약이다. 각 절의 주어자리를 경유해서 이동해야 한다. 다른 주어를 건너갈 수 없다.

B박스 분석 과정

[*Tom*$_i$ appears to Mary [t_2 to be believed by his friends [t_1 to brag about *himself*$_i$]]]

NP 'Tom'은 가장 하위절의 주어자리에서 생성되어 himself과 결속한다. 이어 상위절의 주어자리를 거쳐 마지막 주절의 주어자리로 이동한다. 각 이동에서 다른 주어를 가로질로 이동한 경우는 없다.

풀이 과정에서 어려운 점

복잡한 복문을 제시하여 NP이동 과정을 복잡해 보이도록 했다.

답안

The sentence (5) is syntactically well-formed. The matrix subject originates in the subject position of the lowest clause where theta role is assigned from the predicate 'brag' and the anophor 'himself' is bound, and then the NP 'Tom' moves into the subject position of the middle clauses and then subsequently into the matrix subject position.

과제

- Raising 술어들 암기하기
- anaphor 결속 조건 정리하기

CHAPTER

04

Case Theory

영역	출제년도	내용
1. Case Filter	2008-전국19	
2. Case Assigners	2010-31	verbal/nominal gerund
3. Case in Passivization	2024-A07	passive and raising
4. Case in Raising Predicate		

❑ 연도별 출제빈도

2002	2003	2004	2005	2006	2007	2008	2009	2010	2011	2012	2013	2014	2015	2016	2017	2018	2019	2020	2021	2022	2023	2024	2025	2026
						*		*														*		?

1. 글〈A〉를 읽고 〈B〉에서 비문법적인 문장을 모두 찾아 기호를 쓰고, 비문법적인 이유를 〈A〉의 설명을 바탕으로 쓰시오. 【4 points】 2008-전국19

> Adopting the concepts of traditional grammar, we can say that subjects of finite clauses have Nominative Case and that NPs that are complements of prepositions or verbs appear in the Accusative. Let us postulate that there is a universal requirement that all overt NPs must be assigned abstract Case to satisfy the Case filter.
>
> (1) Case Filter
> Every overt NP must be assigned abstract Case.
>
> To pass the Case filter NPs must be assigned Case by Case assigners such as a finite Tense, a transitive verb, a preposition, or a prepositional complementizer *for*. (the prepositional complementizer can appear in the infinitival clause to assign Accusative Case, since infinitival *to* can't assign Case to the overt subject of an infinitival clause.)
>
> (2) a. He likes her.
> b. She moved toward him.
> c. For her to like him is surprising.

> a. It is likely Mary to be innocent.
> b. I persuaded him to go to college.
> c. She believes sincerely that he is smart.
> d. I don't know whether John to go to the party.
> e. She seems to me to be intelligent.

출제 영역

Case Theory

출제 의도

Case theory의 기본 개념을 묻고 있다. overt NP가 격을 할당받는지 아니면 할당받지 못하는지 문장에서 구분할 수 있어야 한다.

문제 풀이 과정

A박스 요약 및 핵심내용

1. 격여과 조건: Every overt NP must be assigned abstract Case.
2. Case assigners: a finite Tense, a transitive verb, a preposition, or a prepositional complementizer *for*.

B박스 분석 과정

a. It is likely Mary to be innocent.

▶ 'Mary'- caseless; likely 와 to는 case assigner가 아니다.

d. I don't know whether John to go to the party.

▶ 'John'- casekess; whether과 to는 case assigner가 아니다.

풀이 과정에서 어려운 점

답안

The sentences (a) and (d) are ungrammatical. In (a), the NP 'Mary' cannot get case from the adjective 'likely' and the infinitival 'to', and in (d) the NP 'John' cannot get case from the infinitival 'to' and the main verb 'know' due to the interruption of 'whether'.

과제

Case filter와 case assigners 암기할 것

2. Read <A> and <B> and follow the directions. 【2.5 Points】 2010-31

Consider the sentences in (1).

(1) a. John is sure <u>that he will succeed.</u>
    b. John is sure <u>to succeed.</u>
    c. *John is sure <u>his success.</u>

The example (1c) is ungrammatical, though its underlined complement is legitimate. The ungrammaticality of (1c) is attributable to the following constraint on NPs: NPs in sentences should have a case either inherently or through being assigned by finite inflection, a transitive verb, or a preposition. Sentences with a caseless NP are ruled out. In (1c) the underlined complement lacks its case assigner.

a. *The child is difficult to travel alone.
b. *The city's recent dumping the garbage made people upset.
c. *I was pleased my sister to be pregnant.
d. *Not surprisingly did they miss the train.
e. *It turned out the suspect to be innocent.

('*' indicates that the sentence is ungrammatical.)

Choose all the sentences in <B> which have a caseless overt NP.

① a,c,d
② a,c,e
③ b,c,e
④ b,e
⑤ d,e

출제 영역

Case Theory

출제 의도

Case filter를 준수하기 위하여 NP가 격 할당을 받아야 한다. 만약 caseless NP가 문장에 존재한다면 비문처리된다. 이 문제는 단순한 격할당 개념을 넘어 tough movement, passive, raising과 관련된 개념의 배경지식을 요구한다.

문제 풀이 과정

A박스 요약 및 핵심내용

NP는 case assigner에 의해 격을 할당받아야 한다는 핵심 내용언급 : NPs in sentences should have a case either inherently or through being assigned by finite inflection, a transitive verb, or a preposition

B박스 분석 과정

아래 비문 가운데 NP의 caseless로 인한 비문을 선택해야 한다.

a. *The child is difficult to travel alone.

▶ tough construction에서 내포절의 목적어가 주절의 주어자리로 이동해야 하는데 해석상 'the child'는 내포절의 주어이다. 즉 tough 구문을 짝퉁으로 만들어서 비문이다.

b. *The city's recent dumping the garbage made people upset.

▶ 'the garbage'가 caseless하다. dumping과 같은 gerund form은 두 가지 유형으로 구분한다. 하나는 verbal gerund이다. 이 형태는 타동사처럼 뒤에 오는 NP에 격을 할당할 수 있다. 하지만 두 번째 유형인 nominal gerund는 명사로 여겨지므로 뒤의 NP에 격을 할당할 수 없다. 이 문장의 경우에 'recent'라는 형용사가 수식하는 것을 봐서 dumping은 nominal gerund이고 따라서 뒤 NP에 격을 할당할 수 없다.

c. *I was pleased my sister to be pregnant.

▶ 수동화된 동사는 바로 뒤 NP에게 격을 할당하지 않는다. 따라서 NP 'my sister'는 caseless하다.

d. *Not surprisingly did they miss the train.

▶ 부정표현이 문두에 위치할 때 inversion이 발생하는 경우가 많다. 하지만 'not surprisingly'는 '당연하게도'의 의미로 부정어가 포함되어 있지만 부정적 의미를 갖지 않으므로 inversion현상이 일어나지 않는다.

e. *It turned out the suspect to be innocent.

▶ 'turned out'은 seem류의 raising predicate이다. 자동사이므로 case assigner가 아니고 'to'도 격을 할당할 수 없다. 따라서 내포절의 주어인 'the suspect'는 caseless하다.

풀이 과정에서 어려운 점

(b)문장에서 verbal vs nominal gerund 차이에 대한 배경지식을 요구한다.

답안

③

과제

1. verbal vs nominal gerund 차이를 정리한다.
2. passivized verb의 특징을 정리한다.
3. raising construction을 야기하는 술어들을 암기한다.

3. Read the passage in ⟨A⟩ and the examples in ⟨B⟩, and follow the directions. 【4 points】

2024-A07

Passive predicates are known to have no external arguments (i.e., subject arguments). Therefore, the passive sentences in (1) are interpretable but ungrammatical. This is because every sentence requires an overt subject.

(1) a. *_____ is believed that the team will win.
    b. *_____ is believed the team to win.

In this context, the expletive *it*, as a meaningless placeholder, can make (1a) grammatical as shown in (2a). Despite insertion of *it*, however, (2b) still remains ungrammatical. The only difference between (2a) and (2b) is whether the complement clause is finite or non-finite.

(2) a. It is believed that the team will win.
    b. *It is believed the team to win.

Moreover, the same pattern holds in raising predicates as in (3). Note that raising predicates have no external arguments.

(3) a. It seems that the team will win.
    b. *It seems the team to win.

The unexpected parallelism between passive and raising predicates can be accounted for by the empirically-attested observation, which states that a predicate which has no external argument cannot assign accusative/objective(acc/obj) Case. Accordingly, the ungrammaticality of (2b) and (3b) indicates that the NP the team is Case-less because the passive and raising predicates are unable to assign acc/obj Case to it.

This Case-less NP problem can be solved by moving it to the Case-assigned position, such as the subject position of a finite clause or the object position of a transitive verb, without an *it*-insertion:

(4) a. The team is believed to win.
    b. The team seems to win.

Note: '*' indicates the ungrammaticality of the sentence.

a. The detective was thought to have destroyed the evidence.
b. It was told the students that they should pass the exam.
c. It is likely that the mirror should not have been broken.
d. It appeared to be required the students to read two books.
e. The experiment proved to be successful.

Based on ⟨A⟩, identify the TWO ungrammatical sentences containing a Case-less NP in ⟨B⟩. Then explain the common problem with the sentences you chose and its solution without changing the (non-)finiteness of the embedded clauses.

출제 영역

Case Theory

출제 의도

Passive와 Raising구문의 특징을 이해하고 동사 뒤 NP가 D-구조에서 caseless상태이므로 S-구조에서 주절의 주어 자리로 이동하여 tense로부터 격을 할당 받는다는 도출과정을 이해해야 한다.

문제 풀이 과정

A박스 요약 및 핵심내용

1. 수동화된 동사는 internal case를 할당하지 않고, external theta role을 할당하지 않기 때문에 주어 자리가 비워져 있다. 이 주어 자리는 반드시 채워져야 한다. Raising predicate도 동일하다.
   a. Passive predicate의 특징: Passive predicates are known to have no external arguments (i.e., subject arguments).
   b. EPP : every sentence requires an overt subject
2. 동사뒤 caseless NP는 주절의 주어자로 이동하여 격을 할당 받는다.
   This Case-less NP problem can be solved by moving it to the Case-assigned position, such as the subject position of a finite clause.

B박스 분석 과정

b. It was told the students that they should pass the exam.

▶ 'the students'는 수동화된 동사 told로부터 격을 할당받지 못한다. → The students was told that they should pass the exam.

d. It appeared to be required the students to read two books.

▶ 'the students'는 수동화된 동사 required로부터 격을 할당받지 못한다. → The student appeared to be required to read two books.

풀이 과정에서 어려운 점

d. It appeared to be required the students to read two books.에서 raising과 passive가 결합된 문장을 제시해 난이도 상승 의도가 보이나 공부가 된 수험생에게는 '껌'임!

답안

The sentences (b) and (d) are ungrammatical. The passive predicates in (b) and (d) cannot assign accusative case to the NP 'the students' and thus the NP should move to the case-assigned position such as the superficial subject position without an 'it'-insertion.

과제

1. passivized verb의 특징을 정리한다.
2. raising construction을 야기하는 술어들을 암기한다.

CHAPTER

05

Control Theory

영역	출제년도	내용
1. Control	2019-B06	ECM vs Control PRO의 해석
2. PRO theorem (Distribution)		
3. PRO and Binding Theory		
4. PRO and ECM verbs		

❑ 연도별 출제빈도

2002	2003	2004	2005	2006	2007	2008	2009	2010	2011	2012	2013	2014	2015	2016	2017	2018	2019	2020	2021	2022	2023	2024	2025	2026
																	*							?

1. Read the passages and follow the directions. 【5 points】 2019-B06

Despite their similarity on the surface, sentences in (1) are of different types, as suggested in their paraphrasing in (2). Sentence like (1a) are called 'Control' construction; the ones like (1b) 'Raising/ECM' construction. Unlike the latter, an empty pronominal NP PRO is postulated in control constructions.

(1) a. John persuaded Sue to obey her parents.
  b. John believed Sue to be obedient to her parents.

(2) a. John persuaded Sue that she should obey her parents.
  b. John believed that Sue was obedient to her parents.

In fact, there are two kinds of PRO. One is called 'arbitrary PRO', whose meaning is basically "someone" as shown in (3a). Arbitrary PRO is like a referring expression or a pronoun in that it can get its meaning from outside the sentence. The other is 'non-arbitrary PRO', which can be further distinguished into two varieties: 'obligatory control' and 'optional control'. The optional control is exemplified in (3b). PRO here can either refer back to *John* or it can have an arbitrary PRO_{arb} reading. The obligatory control is exemplified in (3c) and (3d): PRO in (3c) obligatorily refers back to the main clause Subject, hence called 'subject control', while PRO in (3d) obligatorily refers back to the main clause Object, hence called 'object control'.

(3) a. [PRO_{arb} to go to college] is not essential for success in life.
  b. $John_i$ knows that it is essential [$PRO_{i/j}$ to be well-behaved].
  c. $John_i$ tried [$PRO_{i/*j}$ to behave].
  d. John persuaded Sue_i [PRO_i to obey her parents].

Note: * indicates the ungrammaticality of the sentence.

(i) a. [PRO to improve himself], John should consider therapy.
  b. John is easy [PRO to talk to].
(ii) a. John motivated Sue to study harder.
  b. John reported Sue to be obnoxious.
  c. John threatened Sue_i to leave her_i.

Based on the description in 〈A〉, first, identify whether PRO in (i a) and (i b) is arbitrary or non-arbitrary, and for non-arbitrary PRO, whether it is obligatory control or optional control. Second, in (ii), identify control constructions only, and then state whether they are subject control or object control.

출제 영역

Control Theory

출제 의도

ECM과 Control구문을 구분할 수 있어야 하고, control 구문에서 PRO가 어떻게 해석되는지 말할 수 있어야 한다. 더불어 tough구문에 대한 기본 배경지식을 요구하고 있다.

문제 풀이 과정

A박스 요약 및 핵심내용

1. Control construction vs. Raising/ECM construction: control verb 뒤 NP는 동사의 목적어이고, ECM verb 뒤 NP는 내포절의 주어이다.

2. PRO의 해석에 따른 유형구분

Arbitrary PRO

Non-arbitrary PRO - obligatory control : subject control / object control

- optional control

B박스 분석 과정

(i) a. [PRO to improve himself], John should consider therapy.

b. John is easy [PRO to talk to].

(i a)의 PRO는 himself의 선행사이고 John으로만 해석되므로 Non-arbitrary PRO이고 obligatory control이다
(i b)는 tough구문으로 John이 전치사 to의 목적어이므로 PRO는 'someone'으로 해석된다. arbitrary PRO이다.

(ii) a. John motivated Sue to study harder.

b. John reported Sue to be obnoxious.

c. John threatened Suei to leave heri.

(ii b)는 ECM이고, 나머지는 control constructiond이다. 동사 뒤 NP가 동사의 목적어로 분석되므로 내포절의 주어는 PRO이다.

풀이 과정에서 어려운 점

(i)에서 PRO의 해석에 혼동을 주었다. (a)는 preposing 구조로, (b)는 tough구문으로 혼동을 야기했지만 도출과정을 이해한다면 함정은 쉽게 피할 수 있다.

답안

PRO in (i a) is non-arbitrary and obligatory in that it gets its meaning from the Subject 'John'. However, PRO in (i b) is arbitrary since its meaning comes from outside the sentence. The sentences (ii a) and (ii c) are control constructions. The former is object control since PRO in the infinitival clause is controlled by the object 'Sue', the latter is object control since PRO is controlled by the subject 'John'.

과제

- ECM과 Control구문 차이점 정리
- PRO의 분포를 이해한다.

CHAPTER

06

Movements

세부영역		출제년도	내용
1. Head Movement	1.1 V to T movement	2022-B02	VtoT & VP-ellipsis
	1.2 T to C movement		
2. NP-movements	2.1 Passivization	2012-21	ECM vs Control (Adjectival passive)
		2007-서울인천-14	ECM/Raising
	2.2 Raising constructions	2006-전국22	sure vs probable
		2009-29	ECM vs Control
		2025-A07	Raising vs Control
		2018-B06	Binding and Raising
	2.3 Ergative/Unaccusative		
3. Wh-movements	3.1 wh-movement		
	3.2 Movement Constraints		
	3.3 Subjacency Condition	2022-B05	
4. Other movements	4.1 Tough movement	2005-전국16	
	4.2 Quantifier Movement		
	4.3 Extraposition	2019-A09	

❑ 연도별 출제빈도

2002	2003	2004	2005	2006	2007	2008	2009	2010	2011	2012	2013	2014	2015	2016	2017	2018	2019	2020	2021	2022	2023	2024	2025	2026
			*	*	*		*			*						*	*			**			*	?

1. Read the passage and follow the directions. 【2 points】 2022-B02

> The tense-affix, such as *-ed* or *-s*, forms an independent head (T) that is separated from a verb in the underlying structure, as shown in (1) and (2). The T-affix needs to attach to a verb in the surface structure via so-called 'Head Movement.' To be specific, T lowers onto lexical verbs, and auxiliary verbs *be* / *have* raise to T.
>
> (1) a. Joe finished the cake.
>   b. [$_{\text{TP}}$ Joe T -ed [$_{\text{VP}}$ finish the cake]]
>
> (2) a. Joe was listening to music.
>   b. [$_{\text{TP}}$ Joe T -ed [$_{\text{VP}}$ be listening to music]]
>
> Let us now observe the data in (3) and (4) that involve so-called 'Verb Phrase ellipsis (VP-ellipsis).' VP-ellipsis is assumed to be licensed when the verb phrase in the second conjunct is isomorphic to that of its corresponding antecedent. For example, the VP of the second conjunct in (3a) is identical to the one in the first conjunct, and deletion of the VP is possible in (3b). The same holds of (4b). However, an interesting difference is observed; namely, dummy *do* is required in the second conjunct in (3), but prohibited in (4).
>
> (3) a. Joe didn't finish the cake, but Mary finished the cake.
>   b. Joe didn't finish the cake, but Mary did 〈~~finish the cake~~〉.
>   c. *Joe didn't finish the cake, but Mary 〈~~finished the cake~~〉.
>
> (4) a. Kim wasn't listening to him, but Sue was listening to him.
>   b. Kim wasn't listening to him, but Sue was 〈~~listening to him~~〉.
>   c. *Kim wasn't listening to him, but Sue did 〈~~be listening to him~~〉.
>
> *Note 1*: '*' indicates the ungrammaticality of the sentence.
> *Note 2*: Strike through inside angled brackets indicates deletion.

Fill in the blanks ① and ② in the correct order with the TWO syntactic operations from the passage.

> To derive (3b) and (4b) and prevent the derivation of (3c) and (4c), a certain order of syntactic operations must take place. For (3b), ___①___ must take place prior to ___②___, but for (4b), ___②___ must take place prior to ___①___.

출제 영역

Head movement

출제 의도

Head movement에서 affix movement와 V to T movement 두 가지 유형이 있고 전자는 일반동사에 적용되고, 후자는 have나 be같은 aux에 적용된다. 이 내용을 VP-ellipsis와 연계하여 상황에 따라 두 규칙이 적용되는 순서가 달라진다는 점을 응용할 수 있어야 한다.

문제 풀이 과정

A박스 요약 및 핵심내용

1. Head movement : T lowers onto lexical verbs, and auxiliary verbs *be* / *have* raise to T.
2. VP-ellipsis : VP-ellipsis is assumed to be licensed when the verb phrase in the second conjunct is isomorphic to that of its corresponding antecedent.

B박스 분석 과정

3b. Joe didn't finish the cake, but Mary did ⟨~~finish the cake~~⟩.

▶ (3b)는 VP-ellipsis가 먼저 일어나야 한다. Head movement가 먼저 일어난다면 finished가 된다.

4b. Kim wasn't listening to him, but Sue was ⟨~~listening to him~~⟩.

▶ (4b)에서 be가 T자리로 이동하여 was가 되는 head movement가 먼저 일어나야 한다. VP-ellipsis가 먼저 일어나면 Sue did ⟨~~be listening to him~~⟩와 같이 비문이된다.

풀이 과정에서 어려운 점

예시를 보고 두 규칙의 순서를 적용하는 과정에서 살짝 머리를 써야한다.

답안

① VP-ellipsis ② Head Movement

과제

- '트포' 8.2 V-movement를 읽고 정리한다.

2. 다음 예문을 보면 sure와 probable은 동일한 유형의 형용사로 보이지만 차이점이 있다. 그 차이점을 통사적 근거를 들어 쓰시오. 【3 points】 2006-전국22

It is sure that John will pass the test. It is probable that John will pass the test.

출제 영역

NP-movement 〉 Raising Construction

출제 의도

Subject to Subject Raising(SSR)

문제 풀이 과정

sure는 subject to subject raising 술어이고 probable은 raising 술어가 아니라는 점을 파악해야 한다.

It is sure that John will pass the test.

→ John is sure to pass the test 구조로 변경가능하지만,

It is probable that John will pass the test.

→ *John is probable to pass the test.로 변경 불가능!

풀이 과정에서 어려운 점

Raising predicate을 사전에 암기했다면 쉽지만 그렇지 않다면 probable과 sure 차이점이 바로 생각해 내는건 쉽지 않다.

답안

The sentence containing the adjective 'sure' can be paraphrased in a sentence that has an infinitival embedded clause as in (1b), but the sentence of (3b) cannot. The adjective 'sure' is a raising predicate, and the subject NP of the infinitival clause moves into the subject position of the main clause.

과제

- Subject-to-Subject raising predicates 정리 및 암기!
- Subject-to-Object raising predicates 정리 및 암기!

3. Read the following and answer the question. 【2 points】 2009-29

> Compare the two sets of sentences in (1) and (2).
>
> (1) a. John was said to have solved all of the questions.
>   b. John was told to solve all of the questions.
>
> (2) a. The earthquake was said to have hit the city.
>   b. *The earthquake was told to hit the city.
>
> The two sentences in (1) contain an NP-movement; an NP moves from the position after the main verb to the subject position. The subject can be interpreted as identical with that of *to*-infinitive. We may assume that the verbs *say* and *tell* take the same type of complement. This assumption, however, cannot be tenable because of the contrast shown in (2). The contrast indicates that the subject in (2a) is not selected by the verb, *say*, while that in (2b) must be selected by the verb *tell*.
>
> Here are some more examples whose structure is identical either with (1a)-type construction or with (1b)-type construction as discuss above.
>
> a. The gladiators were supposed to survive brutal fights.
> b. The passengers were reminded to fasten their seat belts.
> c. The Amish people are reported to live and dress very simply.
> d. The company's workers were found to have organized a union.
> e. The flood victims were advised to prepare food in hygienic conditions.
> f. The listeners were invited to see the world in a different perspective.

Which of the following correctly classifies the above examples a~f?

	(1a)-type	(1b)-types
①	a, b, c	d, e, f
②	a, c, d	b, e, f
③	b, d, e	a, c, f
④	b, d, f	a, c, e
⑤	c, e, f	a, b, d

출제 영역

NP-movement

출제 의도

이 문제는 예외절(exceptional clause)과 통제구문(control construction)을 구별하는 능력을 평가하는 것이다. (1)의 문장에서 주절의 주어는 모두 John으로 동일하지만, (b)에서는 주어가 'the earthquake'로 바뀌었을 때 문법성이 달라진다. 이는 주절의 주어가 표층구조에서 동사 뒤에서 생성된다는 점과 관련이 있다. 이때 동사 뒤의 명사구(NP)가 내포절의 주어인지, 아니면 주절 동사의 목적어인지를 정확히 구별할 수 있어야 한다. 따라서 이 문제는 학습자가 예외절과 통제구문을 올바르게 분석하고 구분할 수 있는지를 묻고 있다.

문제 풀이 과정

- 지문에서 1a-type은 ECM동사를 말한다. ECM동사는 2항술어로 동사 뒤 NP는 내포절의 주어이고 이 NP는 주절의 동사가 수동화되면 주절의 주어자리로 이동한다. ECM동사들은 암기해야 한다.
  a. The gladiators were supposed to survive brutal fights.
  c. The Amish people are reported to live and dress very simply.
  d. The company's workers were found to have organized a union.
- 지문에서 1b-type은 3항을 필요로하는 control 동사를 말한다. 동사 뒤 NP는 목적어이고 내포절의 주어는 PRO가 위치한다. 동사뒤 NP는 동사의 목적어이므로 수동화 구문에서 주어자리로 이동한다.
  b. The passengers were reminded to fasten their seat belts.
  e. The flood victims were advised to prepare food in hygienic conditions.
  f. The listeners were invited to see the world in a different perspective.
- 위 두 유형의 차이점은 동사 뒤 NP가 주절 동사의 논항인지 여부이다.

풀이 과정에서 어려운 점

ECM와 Control 구문을 구분할 때 동사를 통해 알 수 있다. 동사의 특징을 파악할 수 없다면 어렵게 느껴질 수 있다. 따라서 ECM 동사들을 암기하고 있는 것이 좋다.

답안

②

과제

- ECM동사 정리 및 암기!
- Selectional restriction 개념 이해!

4. Read the following and answer the question. 【2.5 points】 2012-21

> Sentence (1) seems to have the same structure as sentence (2).
>
> (1) The researchers appeared to start their project.
> (2) The researchers planned to start their project.
>
> A close analysis, however, would show sentence (1) is different from sentence (2) in the source of the thematic role of the subject *the researcher*. The subject acquires its thematic role from the predicate of the complement clause *start* in sentence (1), but from the predicate of the main clause *planned* in sentence (2). Some of the sentences below show the same pattern of assigning a thematic role to the subject as sentence (1).
>
> a. The manager preferred to please his staff.
> b. The man was relieved to see his son safe.
> c. The angry crowd is unlikely to leave the plaza.
> d. The candidate was keen to resign and support his opponent.
> e. The supervisors turned out to be under investigation.
> f. The children were found to have rashes.

Which of the following lists all and only sentences which show the same pattern as sentence (1)?

① a, b
② a, d, f
③ b, c, d
④ c, e
⑤ c, e, f

출제 영역

NP-movement 〉 Raising vs Control

출제 의도

Raising과 control 구문을 구분하는 문제이다. 이 두 구문은 겉보기에 유사하지만 그 도출과정이 다르기 때문에 통사론에서 출제 유형으로 선호된다.

문제 풀이 과정

- 아래 문장에서 'is unlikely', 'turned out', 'were found'는 raising predicate으로 술어 뒤 NP는 내포절의 주어로 내포절의 술어로부터 의미역을 할당받는다. 이 NP는 격을 할당받기 위해 주절의 주어자리로 이동한다.
  c. The angry crowd *is unlikely* to leave the plaza.
  e. The supervisors *turned out* to be under investigation.
  f. The children *were found* to have rashes.
- 아래 문장의 술어들 'preferred', 'was relieved', 'was keen'은 2할 술어로 주절의 주어는 그 자리에서 생성되어 동사로부터 의미역을 받는다. 이때 내포절의 주어는 PRO가 위치한다. 이러한 구문을 control 구문이라 부른다.
  a. The manager *preferred* to please his staff.
  b. The man *was relieved* to see his son safe.
  d. The candidate *was keen* to resign and support his opponent.

풀이 과정에서 어려운 점

b. The man *was relieved* to see his son safe.에서 relieved가 adjectival passive라는 점을 알아야 한다. adjectival passive의 주어는 이동하지 않고 그 자리에서 생성된다. 따라서 내포절 to see his son safe의 주어는 PRO이다.

답안

⑤

과제

- Subject to Subject Raising 술어 정리 및 암기!
- Verbal passive와 Adjectival passive 차이점 정리!

5. Read the passage and follow the directions. 2007-서울인천-14

Examples (1) and (2) show that the verb believe may take as its complement a finite clause, as in (1), or a non-finite clauses, as in (2).

(1) John believes [that Bill is taller than him].
(2) John believes [Bill to be taller than him].

Complement-taking gets more complicated with the adjective *likely*: It can take a finite clause as its complement, as in (3). But, can it take a non-finite clause complement?

(3) It is likely [that Bill is taller than him].
(4) It is likely [Bill to be taller than him].
(5) Bill is likely [to be taller than him].

Since (4) is ungrammatical, we are tempted to say that the adjective cannot take a ___①___ as its complement. We can't do so, however, because (5) is acceptable. Hence, let us say that *likely* can take a non-finite clause complement, but it cannot allow an NP like *Bill* to immediately follow it. Then, what about the verb *believe* in (2)? Well, we have to say that the verb allows an NP to immediately follow it.

At this point, let us think about the passive past participle of the verb *believe*. Compare (6) and (7) with (1) and (2), respectively.

(6) It is believed [that Bill is taller than him].
(7) It is believed [Bill to be taller than him].

It is interesting to see that it is not the case that both (6) and (7) are okay, ...

(1) Fill in the blank ① with two words from the passage.

(2) Write down the correct version of any ungrammatical sentence in (6) and (7), preserving their (non-)finiteness.

출제 영역

NP-movement 〉 Passivization

출제 의도

ECM과 Raising 구문을 이해해야 한다. ECM동사가 수동화되면 Raising 구문과 유사한 통사적 속성을 보인다. ECM동사가 수동화되면 Raising구문에서처럼 내포절의 주어가 격을 받기 위해서 주절의 주어자리로 반드시 이동해야 한다.

문제 풀이 과정

문장(7)이 비문이다. 내포절의 주어 NP 'Bill' 때문이다. 이 NP는 앞의 동사 believe가 수동화되면서 격을 할당 받을 수 없기때문에 주어자리로 이동해서 격을 할당 받아야 한다. 하지만 주어자리에 허사 'it'이 차지하고 있기 때문에 그 자리로 이동할 수 없어 격여과(case filter)조건을 위반하여 비문처리된다.

(6) It is believed [that Bill is taller than him].
(7) It is believed [Bill to be taller than him].

풀이 과정에서 어려운 점

답안

(1) non-finite clause
(2) The correct version of (7) is 'Bill is believed to be taller than him'.

과제

- ECM동사들 암기!
- Subject to Subject raising 술어들 암기!
- 동사의 수동화시 통사적 속성 이해

6. Read the passage and follow the directions. 【4 points】 2025-A07

> In general, the matrix subject is semantically associated with the matrix verb, which is called an ordinary subject. In (1a), Chris experienced the feeling of wanting to convince Max. In some cases, the matrix subject does not have a direct semantic relationship with the matrix verb, but semantically it belongs solely in the embedded clause. This is called a raised subject. The meaning of (1b) is very close to that of *Chris seemingly convinced Max.*
>
> (1) a. Chris wanted to convince Max.
>   b. Chris seemed to convince Max.
>
> There are diagnostic tests to distinguish one from the other, which include using meaningless dummy pronouns and voice transparency. First, a dummy pronoun, such as *there* or *it*, cannot appear in the ordinary subject position, as shown in (2a), which suggests that the subject of *want* is an ordinary subject. In contrast, the pronoun can appear in the raised subject position, so the appearance of *there* in (2b) suggests that the subject of *seem* is a raised subject.
>
> (2) a. *There wants to be plenty of time.
>   b. There seems to be plenty of time.
>
> The second diagnostic test involves voice transparency between active and passive forms, and only the sentence with a raised subject can denote the same meaning with its passive counterpart. Consider the sentences (3a) and (3b), which are the passive counterparts of (1a) and (1b), respectively.
>
> (3) a. Max wanted to be convinced by Chris.
>   b. Max seemed to be convinced by Chris.
>
> Note that (3a) does not share the same truth condition with (1a) as the subject of *want* refers to *Max* in (3a) but Chris in (1a). In contrast, (3b) is logically equivalent to (1b). Thus, the test results for voice transparency demonstrate that the subject of *want* is an ordinary subject and that of *seem* is a raised subject. Now, consider the sentences (4a) and (4b).
>
> (4) a. The fire fighter attempted to save the man.
>   b. The fire fighter happened to save the man.
>
> The two diagnostic tests can reveal that (4a) contains a(n)①________ subject and (4b) contains a(n) ②________ subject.
>
> *Note*: '*' indicates the ungrammaticality of the sentence.

Fill in the blanks ① and ② each with the ONE most appropriate word from the passage, in the correct order. Then, first, for the raised subject in (4), explain your answer by providing a sentence with a meaningless dummy, using the structural frame, 'to rain'. Second, for the ordinary subject in (4), explain your answer by providing a sentence, using voice transparency.

출제 영역

NP movement 〉 Raising vs Control

출제 의도

Raising과 Control 구문은 유사한 표층구조를 보일 수 있다. 하지만 심층구조가 다르다. 이 차이점을 알고 있어야 한다.

문제 풀이 과정

A박스 요약 및 핵심내용

1. ordinary subject과 raised subject의 차이점을 나타낸다. 주어가 동사의 논항인지 아닌지에 따라 구분하고 있다. (1a)의 주어 Chris는 wanted의 논항이고, (1b)의 주어는 seemed가 아닌 convince의 논항이다.
2. ordinary subject과 raised subject인지 허사 'there'대체로 test 할 수 있다. 표층주어가 want의 논항이라면, 즉 ordinary subject이라면 there로 대체될 수 없다. 하지만 seems의 표층주어는 seem의 논항이 아니므로 there 대체가 가능하다.
3. ordinary subject과 raised subject인지 알기 위해 수동태 변형 test를 할 수 있다.
   내포절의 수동화가 능동의 의미와 같다면 raised subject이고 다르다면 ordinary subject으로 구분할 수 있다.

B박스 분석 과정

(4)의 데이터를 통해 ordinary subject와 raised subject를 파악해야 한다. 이를 위해 지문에서 언급된 두 가지 테스트를 이용해 설명할 수 있어야 한다. (4a)의 attempted는 주어 자리에 논항(argument)을 요구한다. 즉, 이는 ordinary subject에 해당한다. 이를 수동화 테스트(예: *The man attempted to be saved by the firefighter*)를 통해, 능동 구조와 수동 구조 간의 의미 차이로 설명할 수 있다. 반면, (4b)의 동사 happened는 전형적인 raising verb로, 주어 자리가 논항 자리가 아니다. 따라서 *It happened to rain*과 같은 구조에서 주어 자리에 허사(it)를 사용하는 것이 가능하며, 이를 통해 raised subject임을 설명할 수 있다.

풀이 과정에서 어려운 점

답안

ordinary, raised
The dummy pronoun 'it' appears in 'It happened to rain,' but not in 'It attempted to rain,' indicating that the subject of 'happened' is a raised subject. In contrast, (4a) does not share the same truth conditions as its passive counterpart, 'The man attempted to be saved by the firefighter,' showing that the subject of 'attempted' is an ordinary subject.

과제

- Raising (SSR)술어들 암기와 Raising 구조의 특징 정리하기

7. Read the passages and follow the directions. 【5 points】 2018-B06

Sentences must satisfy various principles to be grammatically correct. Consider the following sentence.

(1) a. It seems that Tom admires Mary.
    b. *Tom seems that he admires Mary.

Sentence (1a) is grammatical but sentence (1b) is ungrammatical since the matrix subject *Tom* has no theta role.

Next, consider sentences containing an anaphor.

(2) a. Tom thinks that Mary_i admires herself_i.
    b. *Tom_i thinks that Mary admires himself_i.

(3) a. Tom expects Mary_i to admire herself_i.
    b. *Tom_i expects Mary to admire himself_i.

Sentences (2a) and (3a) are grammatical since the reflexive pronoun *herself* is in the same clause as, and bound by, the antecedent *Mary*. However, sentences (2b) and (3b) are ungrammatical since the reflexive pronoun *himself* does not occur in the same clause as the antecedent *Tom*, violating the binding condition, which requires a reflexive pronoun to be bound by its antecedent in its binding domain, which is the smallest clause containing the anaphor.

Finally, consider the following sentences.

(4) a. It seems that Tom is believed to admire Mary.
    b. *Tom seems that it is believed to admire Mary.

Sentence (4a) is grammatically correct since no violation of grammatical principles has occurred. However, sentence (4b) is ungrammatical since the movement of the matrix subject has violated a constrain which bans a subject from crossing another subject.

Consider the following sentence.

(5) Tom_i appears to Mary to be believed by his friends to brag about himself_i.

In the above sentence, the reflexive pronoun *himself* is in the lowest embedded clause, whereas its antecedent *Tom* is in the subject position of the matrix clause.

State whether sentence (5) in 〈B〉 is syntactically well-formed or ill-formed. Then, explain why, discussing whether the matrix subject can be assigned a theta role, whether it violates any movement constraint, and whether the anaphor can be bound.

출제 영역

NP-movement

출제 의도

NP-movement가 적용되는 과정을 묻는다. 결속이론과 의미역할당 개념이 결합되었지만 NP이동 과정을 정확하게 이해한다면 다른 연계 개념은 어렵지 않다. NP가 생성된 위치를 알아야 하고 그 곳에서 NP이동 제약 ('a constraint which bans a subject from crossing another subject')을 위반하지 않고 최종 목적지인 주절의 주어자리로 이동하는 과정을 말할 수 있어야 한다.

문제 풀이 과정

A박스 요약 및 핵심내용

〈A〉에서 세가지를 언급한다. 첫째, seem류 동사의 논항구조이다. 즉, raising predicate를 언급한다. 내포절의 주어가 주절의 주어자리로 이동해야 한다. 둘째, reflexive는 동일절의 선행사와 결속해야 한다는 결속조건을 언급한다. 통사론에서 매우 중요하고 기본적인 개념이므로 꼭 숙지해야 한다. 마지막으로 NP-이동의 제약이다. 각 절의 주어자리를 경유해서 이동해야 한다. 다른 주어를 건너갈 수 없다.

B박스 분석 과정

[*Tom*$_i$ appears to Mary [t_2 to be believed by his friends [t_1 to brag about *himself*$_i$]]]

NP 'Tom'은 가장 하위절의 주어자리에서 생성되어 himself과 결속한다. 이어 상위절의 주어자리를 거쳐 마지막 주절의 주어자리로 이동한다. 각 이동에서 다른 주어를 가로질로 이동한 경우는 없다.

풀이 과정에서 어려운 점

복잡한 복문을 제시하여 NP이동 과정을 복잡해 보이도록 했다.

답안

The sentence (5) is syntactically well-formed. The matrix subject originates in the subject position of the lowest clause where theta role is assigned from the predicate 'brag' and the anophor 'himself' is bound, and then the NP 'Tom' moves into the subject position of the middle clauses and then subsequently into the matrix subject position.

과제

- Raising 술어들 암기하기
- anaphor 결속 조건 정리하기

8. Read the passage and follow the directions. 【4 points】 2022-B05

Subjacency is a syntactic constraint that restricts movement to be local; namely, movement should cross over only one bounding node (i.e., TP, NP, or CP). Crossing over more than one bounding node in one cycle of movement would result in ungrammaticality. Let us consider the example in (1a), whose derivation is presented in (1b).

(1) a. *What did Sue hear the rumor that Bill broke?

b. *What did $[_{TP}$ Sue hear $[_{NP}$ the rumor $[_{CP}$ t_{WH}' that $[_{TP}$ Bill broke $t_{WH}]]]]$?

The *wh*-phrase in (1) involves two cycles of *wh*-movement. In the first cycle, the *wh*-phrase raises from the complement of *broke* to the specifier of CP in the embedded clause, from which it raises to the matrix specifier position of CP in the second cycle. It is crucial to note that the second cycle crosses over three bounding nodes. This is a violation of Subjacency and ungrammaticality results. Now consider a grammatical sentence in (2), which involves one cycle of *wh*-movement crossing over two TPs, hence apparently violating Subjacency.

(2) Which book does $[_{TP}$ John seem $[_{TP}$ to like $t_{WH}]]$?

To explain the grammaticality of the example in (2), an additional condition in (3) should be imposed for one of the TPs not to be counted as a bounding node.

(3) Complements of a verb are not bounding nodes.

Bearing the above description in mind, let us reconsider sentence (1). When what undergoes the second cycle of wh-movement in (1), it crosses over two bounding nodes. This is because the __________ phrase is no longer a bounding node.

Note: '*' indicates the ungrammaticality of the sentence.

(i) Which actress did you think that John had a strong influence on $\underline{t_{WH}}$?
(ii) Which actress did a picture of $\underline{t_{WH}}$ scare the entire population?
(iii) Which actress did John believe $\underline{t_{WH}}$ spoiled the whole movie?

Fill in the blank in 〈A〉 with a part of speech. Then, based on 〈A〉, identify ONE ungrammatical sentence in 〈B〉, and explain how the sentence violates Subjacency by specifying the bounding nodes that the wh-phrase crosses over.

출제 영역

wh-movement

출제 의도

이동제약인 subjacency condition에 대한 문제이다. 각 이동 사이클마다 이 조건을 준수해야 한다. bounding node가 NP, TP, CP이고 이것들이 동사의 complement일 때는 bounding node가 아니다라는 조건만 주의하면 풀 수 있는 문제이다.

문제 풀이 과정

A박스 요약 및 핵심내용

하위인접조건 설명

1. Subjacency is a syntactic constraint that restricts movement to be local; namely, movement should cross over only one bounding node (i.e., TP, NP, or CP). Crossing over more than one bounding node in one cycle of movement would result in ungrammaticality.
2. Complements of a verb are not bounding nodes.

B박스 분석 과정

(i) [CP Which actress did [TP you think [<u>CP</u> that [TP John had [<u>NP</u> a strong influence on t_{WH}]]]]?

▶ which actress는 첫 번째 내포절 CP의 specifier자리로 이동한 후 문두로 이동한다. 이때 밑줄친 CP와 NP는 동사의 complement이므로 bounding node가 되지않는다. 그러므로 각 이동 사이클에서 하나의 bounding node TP만 건넜으므로 정문이다.

(ii) [CP Which actress did [TP [NP a picture of t_{WH}]scare the entire population]]?

▶ 'which actress'가 t자리에서 문두로 이동할 때 TP와 NP를 한번에 넘어가서 비문이다.

(iii) [CP Which actress did [TP John believe [<u>CP</u> [TP t_{WH} spoiled the whole movie]]]]?

▶ which actress는 두 사이클을 통해 이동한다. 첫 번째 내포절의 spec, CP자리로 이동한 후 문두로 이동한다. 두 번째 사이클에서 밑 줄친 CP가 동사의 complement이므로 bounding node가 아니다. 따라서 각 이동 사이클에서 TP만을 건넜으므로 정문이다.

풀이 과정에서 어려운 점

먼저 각 bounding node(NP, TP, CP)를 정확하게 표시해야 한다. 그리고 동사의 complement가 되는 것은 bounding node가 아니므로 이것을 잘 계산하며 이동 과정을 계산하는 것이 중요한다. 특히 많이 실수하는 부분인데 bounding node를 건넜다는 의미는 그 성분 안에서 나왔다는 의미이다. 그 성분을 그냥 지나갔다는 의미가 아니다.

답안

noun

The sentence (ii) is ungrammatical. The wh-phrase, 'which actress' involves one cycle of movement and it is extracted out of the subject noun phrase, crossing the two bounding nodes, NP and TP.

과제

wh-movement 이동에 관한 예문에서 CP, TP, NP를 표시하는 연습을 하자.

9. Read the passages and follow the directions. 【4 points】 2019-A09

Clausal modifiers of NPs which function as the Subject or the Object can move to the end of the sentence, which is called 'extraposition', as shown in (1) and (2), respectively. The extraposed CP can be adjoined to VP or TP.

(1) a. A man [who has red hair] just came in.
    b. A man just came in [who has red hair].
(2) a. John won't turn a friend [who needs help] away.
    b. John won't turn a friend away [who needs help].

Let's take a closer examination of the extraposition of the CP from the Object position in (2b). As confirmed in (3), VP preposing can be further applied to (2b) and the resulting sentence is grammatical. This suggests that the extraposed CP from the Object position in adjoined to VP, since only phrasal constituents can move.

(3) John said that he wouldn't turn a friend away who needs help, and [turn a friend away who needs help] he won't.

The whole process can be represented as in (4): from the structure in (4a) the clausal modifier CP adjoined to VP in (4b) and the resulting VP constituent moved to the front of the sentence in (4c).

(4) a. [$_{\text{TP}}$ John won't [$_{\text{VP}}$ turn [$_{\text{NP}}$ a friend [$_{\text{CP}}$ who needs help]] away]]
    b. [$_{\text{TP}}$ John won't [$_{\text{VP}}$ [$_{\text{VP}}$ turn a friend t_i away][$_{\text{CP}}$ who needs help]$_i$]]
    c. [[$_{\text{VP}}$ [$_{\text{VP}}$ turn a friend away][$_{\text{CP}}$ who needs help]]$_j$ [$_{\text{TP}}$ John won't t_j]]

From the brief observation, it can be proposed that an extraposed CP is adjoined to the first phrasal constituent containing the NP out of which it is extraposed.

(i) Few people who knew him$_i$ would work with John$_i$.
(ii) Few people would work with John$_i$ who knew him$_i$.
(iii) Work with John$_i$ who knew him$_i$ few people would.

Based on the proposal in ⟨A⟩, first identify in ⟨B⟩ what syntactic category the extraposed CP in (ii), derived from (i), is adjoined to. Second, state whether the preposing in (iii), derived from (ii), is grammatical or not, and then explain why.

출제 영역

Movement 〉 Extraposition

출제 의도

외치구문은 처음 출제된 문제이다. 일반적으로 외치는 문미로 이동한다고 알고 있지만, 목적어 자리에서 외치되는지 주어자리에서 외치되는지에 따라 외치요소가 위치하는 자리가 달라진다. 이 부분을 구조적으로 정확하게 파악할 수 있는지 묻고 있다.

문제 풀이 과정

A박스 요약 및 핵심내용

1. N을 수식하는 CP가 외치되는 현상
2. 외치된 CP의 위치 :
   - object에서 외치되는 경우 : The extraposed CP from the Object position in adjoined to VP – (3)과 같은 VP preposing으로 증명
   - subject에서 외치된 경우에는 정확한 정보를 주지 않음, 단지 아래 내용을 통해서 TP에 adjoin된다는 것을 알수 있음.
     'The extraposed CP can be adjoined to VP or TP.'
     'an extraposed CP is adjoined to the first phrasal constituent containing the NP out of which it is extraposed.'
   - adjoin이라는 개념도 정확하게 설명하지 않음

▶ 위 내용으로만 봐서, 목적어에서 외치된 CP는 VP에 붙고, 주어에서 외치된 CP는 TP에 붙는다는 것을 파악해야 한다.

B박스 분석 과정

(i) Few people who knew himi would work with Johni.
(ii) Few people would work with Johni who knew himi.
(iii) Work with Johni who knew himi few people would.

1. (ii)에서 외치된 CP가 어디에 붙는가: CP 'who knew him'은 주어에서 외치됐으므로 TP에 adjoin된다.
2. (iii)의 문법성과 그 이유? (iii)는 'Work with John she knew him'이 preposing된 구문 → preposing은 구성성분만 가능하다. → 'Work with $John_i$ who knew him_i'는 성분이 아님 → work with John은 VP성분이지만 'who knew him'은 TP에 adjoin된 요소이므로 두 요소가 하나의 성분이 될 수 없음.

풀이 과정에서 어려운 점

목적어에서 외치된 CP는 VP에 붙고, 주어에서 외치된 CP는 TP에 붙는다는 것이 핵심인데 이 구조를 정확하게 이해하기 어려웠다.

답안

In (ii) the extraposed CP 'who needs help' from the Subject position is adjoined to TP. The sentence (iii) is ungrammatical, since the proposed elements 'work with John who knew him' is not a constituent. The phrase 'work with John' is VP, but the CP 'who knew him' is the phrase that is attached to TP.

과제

(2b)와 〈B〉의 (ii)의 수형도를 그려보고 외치된 요소의 위치를 파악한 수, (iii)문장의 수형도를 그린 후 전치된 요소가 왜 성분이 될 수 없는지 구조로 확인해보자.

10. 형용사 impossible이 술어일 때 구문을 아래와 같이 전환할 수 있다. 이와 같은 통사적 특성을 지닌 형용사 3개를 〈보기〉에서 찾아 쓰시오. 【3 points】 2005-전국16

To play this sonata on the violin is impossible. → It is impossible to play this sonata on the violin. → This sonata is impossible to play on the violin.

boring, eager, likely, merry, obvious, pleasant, sorry, tough

출제 영역

Movement > Tough movement

출제 의도

tough구문에 대한 이해와 그 관련 술어들을 알아야 한다.

문제 풀이 과정

A박스 요약 및 핵심내용

(a)와 같은 문장에서 to 부정사절이 외치될 수 있고 나아가 외치된 절의 목적어가 주절의 주어자리로 이동하는 구문은 tough 구문이다.

a. To play this sonata on the violin is impossible.
b. It is impossible to play this sonata on the violin.
c. This sonata is impossible to play on the violin.

B박스 분석 과정

tough구문을 야기하는 술어는 한정되어 있다. 아래에서 boring, pleasant, tough만이 tough구문을 만들 수 있다.

boring, eager, likely, merry, obvious, pleasant, sorry, tough

풀이 과정에서 어려운 점

tough구문의 술어는 암기해야 한다. eager은 통제구문, likely는 상승구문과 관련이 있지만 나머지는 판단하기가 쉽지 않기 때문이다.

답안

The adjectives 'boring', 'pleasant', and 'tough' belong to the third type, since superficial NP subjects originate in the object position of the infinitival embedded clause and moves into the subject position of the main clause.

과제

Teacher's Grammar 원서에서 tough construction을 야기하는 술어를 모두 적고 암기하자.

PART

II

음운론

CHAPTER

01

Phonetics & Phonology

세부 영역		출제년도	내용
1. Phonetics	1.1 Consonants	2020-A04	/ʧ/
	1.2 Vowels	2019-A05	/æ/
2. Phonology	2.1 Allophones	2012-31	Complementary, Overlapping, Free variation
		2005-전국21	Allophones of /p/
	2.2 Phonemes		
	2.3 Allomorphs	2024-A04	

❑ 연도별 출제빈도

2002	2003	2004	2005	2006	2007	2008	2009	2010	2011	2012	2013	2014	2015	2016	2017	2018	2019	2020	2021	2022	2023	2024	2025	2026
			*							*							*	*				*		?

1. Read the passage and fill in the blank with the ONE most appropriate word. 【2 points】

2020-A04

Diphthongs such as [aɪ] and [aʊ] are vowels that exhibit a change in quality within a single syllable. This is due to tongue movement from the initial vowel articulation toward another. In English, this combinatory sound is considered one vowel, as it behaves as a single unit. That is, the words *hide* [aɪ] and *loud* [aʊ] are monosyllabic, as are *heed* [i] and *hid* [ɪ]. Diphthong vowels are different from two consecutive monophthongs as in *seeing* [siɪŋ] and *ruin* [ɹuɪn], which are counted as two syllables.

A similar phenomenon is also observed among consonant sequences. Consider the following examples where two different consonants occurs together at the end of a word:

(1) a. ninth [nθ], warmth [mθ] b. laughs [fs], twelfth [fθ]
c. maps [ps], width [dθ] d. match [ʧ], badge [ʤ]

When the words in (1) are followed by a word beginning with a vowel, such as *is/are* as in (2), the second member of the consonant sequences in (2a)–(2c) can move to the next syllable:

(2) a. Leaving on the nin<u>th is</u> fine with me. ([nθ] or [[n.θ])
b. His lau<u>ghs are</u> heard from down the hall. ([fs] or [f.s])
c. Ma<u>ps are</u> useful when you travel abroad. ([ps] or [p.s])
d. A mat<u>ch is</u> found in the box. ([ʧ] but not [t.ʃ])

In (2a), for example, the second consonant of the underlined part [nθ] forms a new syllable in fast speech. That is, [θ] in *ninth* is a coda of the syllable, but it can move to the next syllable and in turn, it becomes the onset of [θɪz]. However, this resyllabification does not happen in (2d). That is, (2d) is pronounced [mæ.ʧɪz] and not [mæt.ʃɪz]. This is because English treats them differently: the consonant sequences in (2a)–(2c) are two consonant clusters while the one in (2d) is a single sound. This class of sounds is indeed inseparable just like diphthongs, and a member of this class is called a(n) ________ .

출제 영역

Consonants

출제 의도

이중모음과 파찰음(affricate)은 두 개의 음가로 이루어졌지만 분리될 수 없는 하나의 단위로 기능한다는 점을 알아야 한다.

문제 풀이 과정

1. 이중 모음은 두 개의 음가로 구성되지만 하나의 단위로 취급된다.
2. 자음에도 두 갱의 음가로 구성되지만 하나의 단위로 취급되는 것이 있다. (빈칸 처리)

풀이 과정에서 어려운 점

평이함

답안

affricate

과제

24개의 자음을 모두 나열하고 각 자음 마다 특징을 기술해 보자.

2. Read the passage and fill in the blank with the most appropriate IPA symbol. 【2 points】

2019–A05

Two different definitions are employed for the tense–lax distinction. One is the phonetic definition given in (1).

(1) Phonetic definition

a. A tense vowel has a higher tongue position than its lax counterpart.
b. A tense vowel has greater duration than its lax counterpart.
c. A tense vowel requires a greater muscular effort in production than a lax vowel.

The other is a phonologically defined tense–lax separation in terms of the different kinds of syllables in which the vowels can occur.

(2) Phonological definition

Tense vowels can appear in open syllables with stress while lax vowels cannot.

The distributionally based phonological classification of tense–lax comes into conflict with the phonetically based classification in several respects. First of all, both /oʊ/ and /ɔ/ are tense in the phonological classification while they are separated as tense and lax, respectively, in the phonetic classification. Second, there is a problem with regard to duration, which the phonetically based criterion focuses on. While it is true that several of the lax vowels are short, ________ is not. Indeed, this vowel has equal duration with, or even greater duration than typically long and tense vowels.

출제 영역

Vowels 〉 Tense & Lax

출제 의도

긴장모음와 이완모음을 음성학, 음운론적으로 정의할 수 있다. 이 두 정의가 서로 상충하는 모음이 있다. /ɔ/는 음운론적 정의에 따르면 긴장모음이지만 short vowel로 구분되고, /æ/는 음운론적 정의에 따르면 이완모음이지만 다른 어떤 긴장모음보다 길게 발음된다는 점을 알고 있어야 한다.

문제 풀이 과정

1. Tense vowels의 phonetic definition (긴장모음을 물리적 현상으로 정의)
   a. higher tongue position
   b. greater duration
   c. greater muscular effort

2. Tense vowels의 phonological definition (긴장모음을 분포적 특징으로 정의)
   Tense vowels can appear in open syllables with stress while lax vowels cannot.

3. phonetic 정의와 phonological 정의의 충돌
   a. First of all, both /oʊ/ and /ɔ/ are tense in the phonological classification while they are separated as tense and lax, respectively, in the phonetic classification.
   a. Second, while it is true that several of the lax vowels are short, ________ is not.

풀이 과정에서 어려운 점

- AEP의 tense/lax에 대한 내용을 학습했다면 평이함
- 음소를 표기할 때는 반드시 '/ /'를 사용해야 한다는 점 주의!

답안

/æ/

과제

지문에서 언급된 tense/lax의 phonetic/phonological definitions 암기할 것

3. Read ⟨A⟩ and ⟨B⟩ and follow the directions. 【2 points】 2012-31

> When a sound [X] and a sound [Y] occur in the same environment, we say these sounds are in overlapping distribution. On the other hand, if a sound [X] never appears in any of the phonetic environments in which a sound [Y] occurs, the two sounds are in complementary distribution. When the two sounds in overlapping distribution are not involved in the meaning difference of the word pair, it is termed a free variation. If the two sounds in overlapping distribution contribute to the meaning difference of the word pair, the two sounds are in contrastive distribution. When phonetic realizations of two sounds are in contrast with each other, the two sounds are allophones of different phonemes.

> (a) style [staɪɫ] – latter [lǽɾɚ]
> (b) seat [sit˺] – sit [sɪt˺]
> (c) economy [ɪk^{h}ɑ́nə̃mi] – economy [ɛk^{h}ɑ́nə̃mi]
> (d) fell [fiəɫ] – lake [leɪk]
> (e) hit [hɪt˺] – hint [hɪnt˺]
> (f) ram [ræ̃m] – rang[ræ̃ŋ]
> (g) neither [níðɚ] – neither [náɪðɚ]

Which of the following is a correct statement about ⟨A⟩ and ⟨B⟩?

① The underlined pairs of sounds in each word pair (b) and (e) are in overlapping distribution.
② The underlined pairs of sounds in each word pair (c), (f), and (g) are in complementary distribution.
③ The underlined pairs of sounds in each word pair (a), (d), and (g) are in free variation.
④ The underlined pairs of sounds in each word pair (c), (e), and (f) are in contrastive distribution.
⑤ The underlined pairs of sounds in each word pair (b) and (f) are allophones of different phonemes.

출제 영역

Phonology

출제 의도

Overlapping distribution과 Complementary distribution분포 차이를 이해하고 Overlapping distribution분포를 보이지만 의미차이를 갖는 경우(contrastive distribution)와 의미차이가 없는(free variation)를 구분할 수 있어야 한다.

문제 풀이 과정

A박스 요약 및 핵심내용

1. Overlapping distribution
   a. contrastive distribution – to contribute to the meaning difference
   → allophones of different phonemes
   b. free variation – not involved in the meaning difference
2. Complementary distribution

B박스 분석 과정

(a) style [staɪɫ] – latter [lǽɾɚ] ▶ complementary distribution
(b) seat [sit˺] – sit [sɪt˺] ▶ overlapping distribution 〉 contrastive distribution
(c) economy [ɪkʰɑ́nə̃mi] – economy [ɛkʰɑ́nə̃mi] ▶ free variation
(d) fell [fiəɫ] – lake [leɪk] ▶ complementary distribution
(e) hit [hɪt˺] – hint [hɪ̃nt˺] ▶ complementary distribution
(f) ram [ræ̃m] – rang[ræ̃ŋ] ▶ overlapping distribution 〉 contrastive distribution
(g) neither [níðɚ] – neither [náɪðɚ] ▶ free variation

풀이 과정에서 어려운 점

개념 그 자체는 쉽지만 실제 데이터에 적용할려면 다소 당황스러울 수 있다. (연습필요)

답안

⑤

과제

- complementary distribution을 보이는 단어쌍 10개 적기
- overlapping distribution을 보이면서 contrastive distribution 단어쌍 10개 적기
- overlapping distribution을 보이면서 의미 차이가 없는 free variation 단어쌍 10개 적기

4. 다음 글을 읽고, 빈칸에 알맞은 것을 쓰시오. 【3 points】 2005-전국21

In English, aspirated voiceless stops occur at the beginning of a stressed syllable, as in *pie* and *appear*, but unaspirated voiceless stops are produced when preceded by [s] as in *spy* and *spot*. If [p] is pronounced instead of [p^h] in *pie*, it does not make a difference in meaning since these two phonetically different sounds count as the same thing in English. That is, though they are phonetically distinct, they belong to the same mental representation and correspond to a single mental category, which is phonologically referred to as a ___(1)___. The two stops, [p^h] and [p], are allophones of /___(2)___/.

출제 영역

Allophones 〉 /p/

출제 의도

음소와 이음의 차이점을 이해해야 하고 각 이음의 환경을 알아야 한다.

문제 풀이 과정

1. Allophones of /p/:
   a. Aspirated voiceless stops occur at the beginning of a stressed syllable: *pie* and *appear*,
   b. Unaspirated voiceless stops are produced when preceded by [s]: *spy* and *spot*.

2. Phoneme vs Allophone
   Though they([p] and [p^h]) are phonetically distinct, they belong to the same mental representation and correspond to a single mental category.

풀이 과정에서 어려운 점

기본 개념 문제로 평이함

답안

(1) phoneme
(2) /p/

과제

- 영어에 24개 자음이 있다. 각 자음의 allophones을 말하고 그 환경을 기술해보자.

(예) /p/ - [p] when preceded by [s]
[p^h] at the beginning of a stressed syllable
...

5. Read the passage and follow the directions. 【2 points】 2024A-04

> In English, the past-tense morpheme is realized in three different phonetic forms. These are shown in the following words.
>
> (1) grabbed [d]　　reaped [t]　　raided [əd]
> 　　hugged [d]　　poked [t]　　gloated [əd]
>
> Also, the morpheme used to express indefiniteness has two phonetic forms—an [ən] before a word that begins with avowel sound and a [ə] before a word that begins with aconsonant sound.
>
> (2) an [ən] orange　　a [ə] building
> 　　an [ən] accent　　.a [ə] car
> 　　an [ən] eel　　a [ə] girl
>
> Another case of this variation is found in pairs of words in (3). The final consonant in the first morpheme changes when a suffix is added. As a result, each of these morphemes has at least two different phonetic forms.
>
> (3) permit[t] – permiss[s]ive　　include[d] – inclus[s]ive
> 　　electric[k] – electric[s]ity　　impress[s] – impress[ʃ]ion
>
> As exemplified in (1) to (3), a morpheme can have variant phonetic forms which are called ____________.

Fill in the blank with the ONE most appropriate word.

출제 영역

Allomorphs

출제 의도

Allopmoohs의 개념을 묻고 있다.

문제 풀이 과정

Allomorphs 개념 소개 및 예시

'A morpheme can have variant phonetic forms which are called allomorphs.

1. The past-tense morpheme is realized in three different phonetic forms:
   (grabbed [d] reaped [t] raided [əd])
2. The morpheme for indefiniteness has two phonetic forms:
   (an [ən] orange a [ə] building)
3. The final consonant in the first morpheme changes when a suffix is added.
   (permit[t] - permiss[s]ive include[d] - inclus[s]ive)

풀이 과정에서 어려운 점

세 번째 경우에 permit[t]과 permiss[s]를 하나의 morpheme으로 생각하고 이를 morpheme의 variant로 여긴다는 것에 익숙치 않음. 이런 현상은 allomorphs가 아닌 접사 추가로 인한 base의 발음변화로 공부했기 때문이다.

답안

allomorphs

과제

- allophones과 allomorphs의 차이점을 말해보자.

CHAPTER

02

Allophonic Rules

세부 영역		출제년도	내용
1. Allophonic Rules	1.1 Aspiration		
	1.2 Unaspiration		
	1.3 Unexploding		
	1.4 Devoicing		
	1.5 Velarization	2019-B02	Realizations of /l/
	1.6 Nasalizaiton		
	1.7 Flapping	2016-B02	Flapping
	1.8 Dentalizaiton		
	1.9 Syllabic consonant	2007-전국6 2022-B04	Syllabic condition
	1.10 Lengthening		
	1.11 Glottalization	2015-A07	Glottalization of /t/
	1.12 Reduced vowel	2017-A03	[ɪ] in reduced syllables
2. Varieties	2.1 Dialects of /oʊ/	2021-B04	[oʊ] vs. [o]

❑ 연도별 출제빈도

2002	2003	2004	2005	2006	2007	2008	2009	2010	2011	2012	2013	2014	2015	2016	2017	2018	2019	2020	2021	2022	2023	2024	2025	2026
					*								*	*	*		*		*	*				?

1. Read the passage and follow the directions. 【4 points】 2019-B02

> The alveolar lateral approximant /l/ presents appreciable differences among different varieties. In British English, we find the clear 'l', which is articulated with the tongue tip in contact with the alveolar ridge, in words such as *like, law, leaf, light*, etc. On the other hand, /l/ is realized as the velarized dark 'l'. which has a quality similar to /u/ with raising of the back of the tongue toward the velum, in words such as *fall, file, belt, milk*, etc. In Welsh English, /l/ is always pronounced as the clear 'l'.
>
> In some varieties of American English (AE). however, the clear 'l' may hardly be found; most commonly, the realizations differ in terms of shades of the dark 'l'. Thus, a dark 'l' is found in words given in (la), a more velarized darker 'l' variety in words in (1b), and the darkest 'l' in words in (1c).
>
> (1) Realizations of /l/ in some AE varieties
> a. dark 'l'
> lip, left, lash, leaf
> b. darker 'l'
> loose, low, lawn, lock
> c. darkest 'l'
> full, bolt, help, hill
>
> In African American Venacular English (AAVE), /l/ may vocalize to [ʊ] as in (2a) and may be deleted as in (2b).
>
> (2) Realization of /l/ in AAVE
> a. vocalization of /l/
> bell [bɛl] or [bɛʊ]
> milk [mɪlk] or [mɪʊk]
> football [fʊtbɔl] or [fʊtbɔʊ]
> children [ʧɪldɹən] or [ʧɪʊdɹən]
> b. deletion of /l/
> help [hɛlp] or [hɛp]
> elm [ɛlm] or [ɛm]
> wolf [wʊlf] or [wʊf]
> twelve [twɛlv] or [twɛv]

Based on the data given in (1a)–(1b), state the environment(s) for dark 'l' and darker 'l', respectively, in some AE varieties. Then based on the data given in (2a)–(2b), state the environment(s) for the vocalization of /l/ and the deletion of /l/, respectively, in AAVE.

출제 영역

Velarization of /l/

출제 의도

다양한 /l/의 변이 환경을 분석해야한다. allophone은 특정 환경에서만 실현되므로 그 환경을 정확하게 분석할 수 있어야 한다.

문제 풀이 과정

BrE, AE, AAVE에서 /l/의 변이를 비교한다.

1. Realizations of /l/ in BrE
   a. clear 'l' : *like, law, leaf, light* ▶ onset position
   b. dark 'l' : *fall, file, belt, milk* ▶ coda position
2. Realizations of /l/ in AE
   a. dark 'l' : *lip, left, lash, leaf* ▶ before front vowels
   b. darker 'l' : *loose, low, lawn, lock* ▶ before back vowels
   c. darkest 'l' : *full, bolt, help, hill* ▶ coda position
3. Realization of /l/ in AAVE
   a. vocalization of /l/ : *bell* [bɛl] or [bɛʊ]
      milk [mɪlk] or [mɪʊk]
      football [fʊtbɔl] or [fʊtbɔʊ]
      children [ʧɪldɹən] or [ʧɪʊdɹən]
   b. deletion of /l/ : *help* [hɛlp] or [hɛp]
      elm [ɛlm] or [ɛm]
      wolf [wʊlf] or [wʊf]
      twelve [twɛlv] or [twɛv]
4. 3의 분석과정
   ▶ (a) vocalization of /l/의 인접조건 정리 : ɛ_#, ɪ_k, ɔ_#, ɪ_d
   (b) deletion of /l/의 인접조건 정리 : ɛ_p, ɛ_m, ʊ_f, ɛ_v
   ▶ 분석: (a)와 같이 /l/이 모음뒤에서 [ʊ]로 모음화되나 뒤에 자음이 [p, m, f, v]라면 deletion된다. [p, m, f, v]는 [k, d]와는 구분해서 분류해야한다. 즉, labials!

풀이 과정에서 어려운 점

Realization of /l/ in AAVE의 데이터 분석이 가장 어렵다. 따라서 4와 같은 분석과정을 연습해야 한다.

답안

Dark 'l' and darker 'l' are found before front vowels and back vowels, respectively in some AE varieties. In AAVE, /l/ is deleted before a labial consonant, otherwise, postvocalic /l/ is vocalized.

과제

Realization of /l/ in AAVE의 분석과정을 데이터만 보고 여러번 연습 해 보자.

2. Read the passage and follow the directions. 【4 points】 2016-B02

In American English, alveolar stops can be pronounced as a flap, which is caused by a single contraction of the muscles so that one articulator is thrown against another. It is often just a very rapid stop gesture. This sound can be written with the symbol [ɾ] so that *fatty* can be transcribed as [fæ´ɾɪ]. <u>Alveolar stops become a flap when they are located between a stressed vowel and an unstressed vowel</u> as in *water* and *header*. In addition to this rule, there are two other rules that account for the contexts where flapping occurs.

autumn, riddle, monitor, saddle, humanity, daddy, battle, comedy, competing

Identify ALL the words from 〈B〉 that cannot be accounted for by the underlined rule in 〈A〉. Then cetegorize them into TWO groups according to their occurrence contexts and state ONE rule for EACH group which accounts for each data set.

출제 영역

Flapping

출제 의도

/t, d/의 flapping 환경을 정확하게 알고 있어야 한다. 이 문제에서 한 가지 조건은 제시하고 나머지 두 조건과 그에 해당하는 단어를 선택해야 한다.

문제 풀이 과정

A박스 요약 및 핵심내용

/t, d/의 flapping 세가지 조건

첫째, Alveolar stops become a flap when they are located between a stressed vowel and an unstressed vowel.

B박스 분석 과정

아래 나머지 두 조건은 이미 알고 있어야 한다. 데이터를 보고 추측할 수 있지만 위험부담이 있다.

둘째, Flapping occurs between a stressed vowel and a syllabic consonant: *riddle, saddle, battle*

셋째, Flapping occurs between unstressed vowels: *monitor, humanity, comedy*

(강세 위치를 정확히 알고 있어야 한다.)

나머지 autumn, daddy, competing은 첫 번째 조건에 속하는 단어들이다.

풀이 과정에서 어려운 점

일반적으로 데이터를 통해 환경을 기술하는 문제가 아니라 환경을 이미 알고 있는 상태에서 그에 해당하는 단어를 고르는 점이 어렵다.

답안

The words 'riddle', 'monitor', 'saddle', 'humanity', 'battle', and 'comedy' cannot be account for by the rule in 〈A〉. For the words 'riddle', 'saddle', and 'battle', flapping occurs between a stressed vowel and a syllabic consonant, and for 'monitor', 'humanity', and 'comedy', flapping occurs between unstressed vowels.

과제

Flapping현상이 적용된 단어들을 AEP에서 찾아 정리하고 발음해 보자. 또한 그 환경도 세부적으로 기술해 보자.

3. 다음 글을 읽고, 빈칸 (1)과 (2)에 들어갈 수 있는 단어를 <보기>에서 각각 2개씩 찾아 그 기호를 쓰시오. 【3 points】 2007-전국6

> It is common that every syllable contains a vowel at its nucleus. However, certain consonants also act as the nucleus elements of syllables in English. Words such as ______, in which the nasal sound comes after stops or fricatives, show that the nasals are syllabic. But we can't say that nasals become syllabic whenever they occur at the end of a word after a consonant. Words such as ______, in which the nasal sound comes after a sonorant consonant, show that the nasals are not syllabic. Therefore, the key issue here appears to be the manner of articulation of the consonant preceding the nasal sound at the end of a word.

(a) charm	(b) chasm	(c) film
(d) seldom	(e) leaden	(f) salon

출제 영역

Syllabic Consonants

출제 의도

Nasals가 syllabic이 되는 조건과 될 수 없는 조건을 제시한 후 그에 해당되는 단어를 찾는 문제이다.

문제 풀이 과정

A박스 요약 및 핵심내용

Nasals의 syllabic 조건 : The nasal sound comes after stops or fricatives, But we can't say that nasals become syllabic whenever they occur at the end of a word after a sonorant consonant.

B박스 분석 과정

1. stop or fricative (obstruent) + Nasal : chasm [kæzm̩], leaden [ledn̩]
2. sonorant + Nasal : charm [ʧɑrm̩], film [film̩]
3. seldom - nasal앞에 stop /d/가 있으나 그 자음 앞에 또 다른 자음 /l/이 존재하므로 syllabic될 수 없음
4. salon - nasal이 포함된 음절에 강세가 위치하므로 syllabic이 될 수 없다.

풀이 과정에서 어려운 점

'seldom'과 'salon'에서 Nasal이 syllabic될 수 없는 조건은 언급되지 않았다. 이 조건은 이미 알고 있어야 한다.

답안

chasm, leaden / charm, film

과제

- Nasals이 syllbic의 될 수 있는 조건과 될 수 없는 환경을 AEP를 참고해 정리한다.
- liquids가 syllbic의 될 수 있는 조건과 될 수 없는 환경을 AEP를 참고해 정리한다.

4. Read the passage and follow the directions. 【4 points】 2022-B04

Nucleus positions in syllables are usually taken by vowels. In the cases that syllables have no vowel, consonants stand as the nucleus. It is usual to indicate that a consonant is syllabic by means of a small vertical mark (̩) beneath or above the symbol. Even though syllabic consonants are observed word-medially (e.g., Hungary [hʌŋgɹ̩i]), most syllabic consonants are found word-finally as in (1). Note that some words can be realized in two phonetic forms.

(1) Syllabic consonants

syllabic [n̩]	syllabic [m̩]	syllabic [ŋ̍]	syllabic [l̩]
open [oʊpn̩]	~[oʊpm̩]		supple [sʌpl̩]
ribbon [ɹɪbn̩]	~[ɹɪbm̩]		rebel [ɹɛbl̩]
cotton [kɑtn̩]			bottle [bɑtl̩]
sudden [sʌdn̩]			muddle [mʌdl̩]
broken [bɹoʊkn̩]		~[bɹoʊkŋ̍]	uncle [ʌŋkl̩]
pagan [peɪgn̩]		~[peɪgŋ̍]	fungal [fʌŋgl̩]
question [kwɛstʃn̩]			satchel [sætʃl̩]
soften [sɔfn̩]			muffle [mʌfl̩]
lengthen [lɛŋθn̩]	anthem [ænθm̩]		lethal [liθl̩]
lesson [lɛsn̩]	handsome [hænsm̩]		muscle [mʌsl̩]
ashen [æʃn̩]			bushel [bʊʃl̩]
column [kɑləm], *[kɑləmn̩]			mammal [mæml̩]
			channel [tʃænl̩]
corn [kɔɹn], *[kɔɹn̩]			peril [pɛɹl̩]
			sale [seɪl], *[seɪl̩]

The table in (2) provides distinctive features to categorize natural classes depending on the manners of articulation.

(2)

	vowels	glides	liquids	nasals	obstruents
[syllabic]	+	−	−	−	−
[consonantal]	−	−	+	+	+
[approximant]	+	+	+	−	−
[sonorant]	+	+	+	+	−

Note 1: '*' indicates a non-permissible form.
Note 2: '~' indicates phonetic variation.

a. In the word-final position, /n/ is realized as a syllabic nasal when immediately preceded by ______ segments.
b. In the word-final position, /l/ is realized as a syllabic liquid when immediately preceded by ______ segments.

Based on the data in (1), fill in each blank in 〈B〉 with the ONE most appropriate feature in (2), respectively. Write your answers in the correct order. Then, identify the syllabic consonant that is always homorganic with the preceding consonant in the given data, and explain the reason.

출제 영역

Syllabic Consonants

출제 의도

Nasals와 liquid /l/의 syllabic 조건을 찾아 그것을 distictive feature로 표현할 수 있어야 한다. 이를 위해서는 소리를 정확하게 분류할 수 있어야 하고 그 분류된 소리의 distictive feature를 찾을 수 있어야 한다. 이 문제는 약간의 배경지식도 필요로 하고 있다.

문제 풀이 과정

A박스 요약 및 핵심내용

1. nasal sounds와 liquid /l/이 syllabic된 data제시
2. manners of articulation을 distinctive features로 나타낸 표 제시

▶ Syllabic 환경을 features로 나타내라는 의도가 보임

B박스 분석 과정

a. In the word-final position, /n/ is realized as a syllabic nasal when immediately preceded by ([-sonorant]) segments.

▶ 분석과정 : nasals 앞에 위치하는 자음을 살펴보고 분류한 후 변별자질로 표현한다.
[p, b, t, d, k, g, ʧ, f, ɵ, s, ʃ]는 가능하지만, [m, r]는 불가능하다 → obstruents가 앞에 위치할 때 가능하므로 [-sonorant]로 정리!

b. In the word-final position, /l/ is realized as a syllabic liquid when immediately preceded by ([+consonantal]) segments.

▶ 분석과정 : liquid /l/ 앞에 위치하는 자음을 살펴보고 분류한 후 변별자질로 표현한다.
[p, b, t, d, k, g, ʧ, f, ɵ, s, ʃ, <u>m, n, r</u>]이 앞에 위치할 때 가능하지만 *[seɪl̩]처럼 모음 뒤에서는 불가하다. → obstruents, nasals, liquids가 앞에 위치할 때 가능하므로 [+consonantal]로 표현!

c. 지문에서 항상 앞 자음과 homorganicity를 보이는 syllabic consonant는 [ŋ̍]이다.

풀이 과정에서 어려운 점

1. /l/앞의 자음에 대한 변별자질이 왜 [+consonantal]이고 [-syllabic]은 안되는가? 데이터에는 glide /j, w/가 syllabic /l/앞에 올 수 없다는 배경지식을 이용해야 한다. (불친절한 지문이다)
2. [ŋ̍]이 항상 앞 자음과 homorganicity를 보이는 이유에 대한 근거를 전혀 제공하지 않는다. (역시 불친절한 지문이다)

답안

[-sonorant], [+consonantal]
The syllabic consonant [ŋ̍] is likely to assimilate to the place of articulation of the preceding consonant in colloquial speech.

과제

1. AEP에서 syllabic consonant 조건을 정리한다.
2. 지문에서 제시된 소리들을 분류하여 distinctive features 표현하는 방법을 연습해야 한다.

5. Read the passage and fill in each blank with ONE word. Write your answers in the correct order. 【2 points】 2015-A07

A glottal stop is the sound that occurs when the vocal cords are held together. In many accents of English, a glottal stop is often realized as a(n) ________ of /t/ in the words given in (1).

(1) Batman catnap
/t/ /t/
butler atlas
/t/ /t/

While the /t/ in the words in (1) can be produced as a glottal stop, the /t/ in the words in (2) cannot be realized as a glottal stop.

(2) atrocious attraction
/t/ /t/
atrophic patrol
/t/ /t/

The data given in (1) and (2) show that, unlike the /t/ in the words in (1), the /t/ in the words in (2) is in a(n) ______ position of a syllable, and thus it cannot be produced as a glottal stop.

Note: In the words in (1) and (2), the underlined spelling of *t* or *tt* represent /t/.

출제 영역

Glottalization

출제 의도

/t/가 glottal stop으로 발음되는 환경을 묻고 있다. /t/ Syllable의 coda에 위치할 때 주로 나타나는 현상이다.

문제 풀이 과정

1. 발음 : A glottal stop is the sound that occurs when the vocal cords are held together.
2. 현상 : A glottal stop is often realized as an allophone of /t/.
3. 환경 : /t/의 음절 위치로 접근 → /t/ can be produced as a glottal stop when it is in a coda position of a syllable.

풀이 과정에서 어려운 점

음운 환경을 말할 때 syllable의 구조로 접근해야 하는 것을 찾는 것이 가장 중요함! (암기보다는 실제 data분석을 해야함)

답안

allophone, onset

과제

/t/의 allophones을 모두 나열할 뒤 그 환경을 모두 기술해 보세요.

6. Read the passage and fill in the blank with ONE word. 【2 points】 2017-A03

While all vowels of English (except [ə]) can occur in stressed syllables, many of these vowels reveal alternations with an [ə] in reduced syllables in morphologically related words as shown in (1).

(1)

Stressed Syllable			Reduced Syllable	
/i/	homogeneous	[hoʊmədʒiniəs]	homogenize	[həmadʒənaɪz]
/eɪ/	explain	[ɪksplein]	explanation	[ɛkspləneɪʃən]
/ɛ/	perpetuate	[pəɹpɛtʃʊeɪt]	perpetuity	[pəɹpətʃuəti]
/ɑ/	demonstrable	[dɪmonstɹəbəl]	demonstration	[dɛmənstɹeɪʃən]
/ʌ/	confront	[kənfɹʌnt]	confrontation	[kɑnfɹənteɪʃən]
/ɑɪ/	recite	[ɹɪsɑɪt]	recitation	[ɹɛsəteɪʃən]

However, it is not uncommon to see an [ɪ] in reduced syllables of the words in (2).

(2) a. selfish [selfɪʃ]
sandwich[sændwɪtʃ]
marriage [mæɹɪdʒ]

b. metric [mɛtɹɪk]
running [ɹʌnɪŋ]
allegation [ælɪgeɪʃən]

In the examples in (2). [ɪ] occurs before palato-alveolars as in (2a) or before ______ as in (2b). (Your answer must account for all three examples in (2b).)

출제 영역

Vowel Reduction

출제 의도

모음의 약화될 때 주로 [ə]로 발음되지만 [ɪ]로 발음되기도 한다. [ə]가 아닌 [ɪ]로 모음이 약화되는 환경을 제시된 데이터를 통해 찾을 수 있어야 한다.

문제 풀이 과정

1. [ə]로 약화되는 모음 : 강세받지 않는 음절에서 약화됨
2. [ɪ]로 약화되는 모음 : 강세받지 않고 /ʃ, ʧ, ʤ, k, ŋ, g/소리 앞에서 [ɪ]로 약화됨

(2) a. selfish [sɛlfɪʃ]
sandwich[sændwɪʧ]
marriage [mæɹɪʤ]
b. metric [mɛtɹɪk]
running [ɹʌnɪŋ]
allegation [ælɪgeɪʃən]

▶ 모음이 [ɪ]로 약화될 때는 모음 뒤 특정한 자음들이 위치할 때이다. 이 자음들(/ʃ, ʧ, ʤ, k, ŋ, g/)은 앞 세 개는 palato-alveolars이고, 나머지 세 개는 velars로 구분된다.

풀이 과정에서 어려운 점

[ɪ]로 약화되는 조건이 무엇인지 정확하게 파악해야 한다. 모음 뒤 특정 자음들을 주목해야 한다.

답안

velars

과제

- 모음에서 reduced vowel의 특징을 AEP를 참고하여 정리하자
- 지문 (1)단어들의 강세 위치를 정리하자

7. Read the passage and follow the directions. 【4 points】 2021-B04

> In a number of American English dialects, /oʊ/ is realized as a diphthong [oʊ] or a monophthong [o].
>
> (1) /oʊ/ is realized as [oʊ].
>
> | | |
> |---|---|
> | a. Poe | [poʊ] |
> | b. low | [loʊ] |
> | c. hope | [hoʊp] |
> | d. coat | [koʊt] |
> | e. most | [moʊst] |
> | f. flow | [floʊ] |
>
> (2) /ou/ is realized as [o].
>
> | | |
> |---|---|
> | a. pole | [pol] |
> | b. Coletrane | [koltrein] |
> | c. hole | [hol] |
> | d, told | [told] |
> | e. mole | [mol] |
> | f. fold | [fold] |
>
> Observing the patterns in (1) and (2), one could make a generalization as in (3).
>
> (3) /ou/ is realized as [o] when it is close to /l/.
>
> However, the generalization in (3) does not always hold for the data above. Moreover, it cannot explain the contrast between (4) and (5) below.
>
> (4) /ou/ is realized as [ou].
>
> | | |
> |---|---|
> | a. low-ly | [loʊli] |
> | b. slow-ly | [sloʊli] |
> | c. low-land-s | [loʊləndz] |
> | d. toe-less | [toʊlas] |
>
> (5) /u/ is realized as [o].
>
> | | |
> |---|---|
> | a goal-ie | [goli] |
> | b. roll-ing | [rolin] |
> | c. bowl-er | [bolər] |
> | d. hole-in-one | [holmwan] |
>
> *Note*: -indicates a morpheme boundary.

> a. shall<u>ow</u>ly b. s<u>o</u>ldier c. <u>oa</u>tmeal d. p<u>ou</u>ltry

In ⟨B⟩, identify TWO words where the underlined /oʊ/ is realized as 【o】 in the dialects of English described in ⟨A⟩. Then, revise the generalization in (3) to account for all the data in ⟨A⟩

출제 영역

Allophones of /oʊ/ in AE

출제 의도

/oʊ/가 환경에 따라 [oʊ]와 [o]로 발음될 수 있다. 즉 [oʊ]와 [o]의 환경을 파악할 수 있어야 한다.

문제 풀이 과정

A박스 요약 및 핵심내용

1. /oʊ/가 [oʊ]실현되는 data (1)과 [o]로 실현되는 data(2)를 제시한다. 이 데이터들의 일반화한 조건(3)을 제시한다. '/ou/ is realized as [o] when it is close to /l/'.
2. 위 일반화가 적절치 않다고 지적하며 추가 데이터를 제시한다.

B박스 분석 과정

1. 먼저, (3)의 일반화를 수정해야 한다.
   a. '... is close to /l/'과 같은 음운 조건은 없다. close to 아닌 선/후행 관계로 기술해야 한다.
   b. (1)의 low [loʊ]나 flow [floʊ]도 /l/과 가까이 위치하지만 [oʊ]로 발음되므로 (3)은 적절치 않다.
      ▶ 'close to'가 아닌 바로 뒤에 위치해야 하므로 immediately followed by로 수정해야 한다.
   c. (4)와 (5)를 살펴보면 후행조건도 불충분하다. /l/이 가까이 위치하지만 [oʊ]로 발음된다.
      ▶ (4)와 (5)는 /l/이 후행하지만 위치한 단위가 다르다는 점을 파악해야 한다. (4)는 모음과 다른 morpheme이고 (5)는 모음과 같은 morpheme이다.
   d. 따라서 아래 data에 의해 다음과 같이 수정해야 한다.
      ▶ /oʊ/ is realized as [o] when it is immediately followed by /l/ within the same morpheme.

2. 수정된 일반화를 기초로 /l/이 바로 뒤에 위치하고 동일한 morpheme에 있는 /oʊ/를 고른다.
   a. shallowly : -ly가 다른 morpheme이다.
   b. soldier : /l/이 후행하며 모음과 동일한 morpheme에 위치한다.
   c. oatmeal : 모음 바로 뒤에 /l/이 위치하지 않는다.
   d. poultry : /l/이 후행하며 모음과 동일한 morpheme에 위치한다.

풀이 과정에서 어려운 점

지문 중간에 일반화한 (3)의 조건에 다른 조건을 추가하는 것이 이전의 유형이다. 하지만 이 문제에서 일반화 조건(3)이 부적절하다는 내용을 언급했으므로(대충 읽었으면 놓칠 수 있다) 이를 수정한 후 추가 조건을 더 붙여야 한다.

답안

The underlined /oʊ/ is realized as [o] in the words, (b) and (d). The revised generalization in (3) is as follows: /oʊ/ is realized as [o] when it is followed by /l/ within the same morpheme.

과제

1. morpheme의 정의를 알고 단어에서 형태소 단위를 구분하는 것을 연습하자.

CHAPTER

03

Phonological Process

세부영역		출제년도	내용
1. Assimilation	1. Voicing assimilation 2. Place assimilation 3. Manner assimilation	2018-A05	Inflectional suffix
		2010-30	Prefix ‘in-’
		2009-34	/t, d, n/
		2008-전국17	Alveolar stops
		2019-A04	‘com-’, ‘con-’
	4. Coalescence	2007-전국12	Palatalization
		2012-33	Palatalization
		2020-A07	Palatalization & Spelling error
2. Dissimilation		2020-B03	‘il/ir-’, ‘-ar/-al’
		2011-33	‘similar’
3. Deletions & Reduction		2017-B03	Schwa
		2015-B03	/j/-dropping
		2006-서울인천11	Function words
		2002-전국15	‘might have thought’
		2024-B04	/r/ deletion
4. Epenthesis		2018-B01	/j/ and /w/
		2005-서울인천23	Plural suffix -*s*
5. Metathesis		2011-35	Speech errors
6. Neutralization		2013-30	Glottal stop of /p, t, k/
7. Morph-phonology		2014-A05 2023-B04	Suffix -*al*
		2025-B06	Suffix -*er*

❑ 연도별 출제빈도

2002	2003	2004	2005	2006	2007	2008	2009	2010	2011	2012	2013	2014	2015	2016	2017	2018	2019	2020	2021	2022	2023	2024	2025	2026
*			*	*	*	*	*	*	**	*	*	*	*		*	**	*	**			*	*	*	?

1. Read the passage and fill in each blank with the ONE most appropriate word, respectively. 【2 points】 2018-A05

> The examples in (1) show that word final consonant clusters formed by the addition of an inflectional suffix undergo voicing assimilation.
>
> | | | | | |
> |---|---|---|---|---|
> | (1) | cats | [kæts] | dogs | [dɔgz] |
> | | cans | [kænz] | bells | [bɛlz] |
> | | baked | [beɪkt] | popped | [pɑpt] |
> | | farmed | [fɑɹmd] | sealed | [sild] |
>
> The examples in (2) illustrate the voicing agreement patterns in word final consonant clusters of the underived lexical items.
>
> | | | | | | | | |
> |---|---|---|---|---|---|---|---|
> | (2) | a. | apse | [æps] | *[æpz] | adze | [ædz] | *[æds] |
> | | | apt | [æpt] | *[æpd] | lift | [lɪft] | *[lɪfd] |
> | | | act | [ækt] | *[ækd] | cast | [kæst] | *[kæsd] |
> | | b. | mince | [mɪns] | *[mɪnz] | belch | [bɛlʧ] | *[bɛlʤ] |
> | | | purse | [pəɹs] | *[pəɹz] | pump | [pʌmp] | *[pʌmb] |
> | | | mint | [mɪnt] | *[mɪnd] | elk | [ɛlk] | *[ɛlg] |
>
> Unlike the lexical items with inflectional suffixes in (1), voicing agreement selectively occurs for the underived lexical items in (2). As can be seen in (2b), there are cases where clusters composed of ________ and ________ do not agree in voicing.

출제 영역

Assimilation

출제 의도

단어 끝의 자음군이 inflectional suffix에 첨가에 의해 생성된 경우는 voicing assimilation이 발생하지만 단어끝 자음군이 underived lexical items에서 형성되었을 경우에는 선택적으로 일어난다. 그 환경을 분석해야 한다.

문제 풀이 과정

1. Word final consonant clusters formed by the addition of an inflectional suffix undergo voicing assimilation.
2. Voicing agreement selectively occurs for the underived lexical items in (2).
   자음군의 구성을 분석해야 한다.

(2a)	p+s	(2b)	n+s
	p+t		r+s
	k+t		n+t
	d+z		l+ʧ
	f+t		m+p
	s+t		l+k

▶ Voicing agreement가 적용되는 (2a)는 obstruents+obstruents이지만, (2b)는 sonorants+obstruents로 구성된다.

풀이 과정에서 어려운 점

해당 자음의 정확한 분류가 중요한다.

답안

sonorants, obstruents

과제

2. Read 〈A〉 and 〈B〉 and follow the directions. 【2 points】 2010-30

Assimilation, one of the most common phonological process, comes in two types. One is place assimilation, in which the assimilated sound becomes similar to the conditioning sound in terms of place. The other is manner assimilation, where a sound takes on the manner of articulation from an adjacent sound. In English, these two types of assimilation can be found in the alternations of the negative prefix 'in-,' as shown below.

(1) /in + kouhiərənt/ → [iŋ kouhɪ´ərənt]

(2) /in + regjələr/ → /irregjələr/ → [ire´gjələr]

(Note: In (2), after assimilation, degemination occurs, i.e., the two identical consonants are fused into one.)

a.	/in + laʤikəl/	'illogical'
b.	/in + mətjuər/	'immature'
c.	/in + rezəlu:t/	'irresolute'
d.	/in + grætətju:d/	'ingratitude'
e.	/in + kərekt/	'incorrect'

Choose all the examples in 〈B〉 which undergo place assimilation in rapid speech.

① a, b, c

② a, c

③ b, c

④ b, d, e

⑤ d, e

출제 영역

Assimilation

출제 의도

Assimilation을 두 가지 유형으로 구분한다. 동화방식에 따라 Place assimilation과 Manner assimilation로 구분할 수 있다. 데이터의 음운현상을 분석하여 이 두 동화 유형을 말할 수 있어야 한다.

문제 풀이 과정

A박스 요약 및 핵심내용

1. Assimilation
   a. Place assimilation : the assimilated sound becomes similar to the conditioning sound in terms of place.
      /in + kouhiərənt/ → [iŋkouhɪ′ərənt]
   b. Manner assimilation : a sound takes on the manner of articulation from an adjacent sound.
      /in + regjələr/ → /irregjələr/ → [ire′gjələr]

▶ [Terms] degemination: the two identical consonants are fused into one.

B박스 분석 과정

a. /in + laʤikəl/ 'illogical' : /n/ → [l] manner assimilation
b. /in + mətjuər/ 'immature' : /n/ → [m] place assimilation
c. /in + rezəlu:t/ 'irresolute' : /n/ → [r] manner assimilation
d. /in + grætətju:d/ 'ingratitude' : /n/ → [ŋ] place assimilation
e. /in + kərekt/ 'incorrect' : /n/ → [ŋ] place assimilation

풀이 과정에서 어려운 점

Place동화인지 manner동화인지 연습해야 한다.

답안

④

과제

문제에 언급된 모든 단어들의 강세위치를 포함하여 발음기호를 두 가지 버전으로 써보자. 하나는 broad transcription, 다른 하나는 narrow transcription.

3. Read 〈A〉 and 〈B〉 and follow the directions. 【2.5 points】 2009-34

〈A〉

The following rules describe some characteristic features of Standard American English.

(1)

The lateral /l/ can be syllabic (i.e. standing as the nucleus of a syllable) following a sequence of a stressed vowel and an alveolar stop (an oral or a nasal stop).

(2)

A word-final /t/, /d/ or /n/ may assimilate in place of articulation to a following word-initial bilabial or velar stop, resulting in two identical consonants in some cases. But some features such as voicing and nasality of the consonant remain constant. When place assimilation results in two identical consonants, it is called total assimilation.

〈B〉

Each sentence below may or may not contain a word/phrase to which rule (1) or (2) in 〈A〉 is applied.

a. Can you pass me the one in the middle?
b. He lost his pet cat yesterday.
c. You excel as a painter.
d. I like the blue soap dish.
e. I will cross the channel by boat.
f. Teachers extol the virtue of honesty.
g. You're a very good boy.
h. I heard that ten cooks went home.

Choose the correct match between each rule in 〈A〉 and the corresponding examples in 〈B〉. For (2) in 〈A〉, find ONLY the examples in which total assimilation occurs.

	(1)	(2)
①	a, c	d, h
②	a, e	b, d
③	a, e	b, g
④	c, f	d, h
⑤	e, f	b, g

출제 영역

Assimilation & Syllabic

출제 의도

두 음운 규칙을 제시하고 그 조건에 해당하는 영어표현을 찾을 수 있어야 한다.

문제 풀이 과정

A박스 요약 및 핵심내용

1. Syllabic : The lateral /l/ can be syllabic following a sequence of a stressed vowel and an alveolar stop (an oral or a nasal stop).
2. A word-final /t/, /d/ or /n/ may assimilate in place of articulation to a following word-initial bilabial or velar stop, resulting in two identical consonants in some cases. (total assimilation)

B박스 분석 과정

a. Can you pass me the one in the middle?	(1) v́+/d/+[l̩]
b. He lost his pet cat yesterday.	(2) /t/→[k]/_/k/ idential - total assimilation
c. You excel as a painter.	
d. I like the blue soap dish.	
e. I will cross the channel by boat.	(1) v́+/n/+[l̩]
f. Teachers extol the virtue of honesty.	
g. You're a very good boy.	(2) /d/→[b]/_/b/ idential - total assimilation
h. I heard that ten cooks went home.	(2) /n/→[ŋ]/_/k/ not idential

풀이 과정에서 어려운 점

a. ⟨A⟩의 음운규칙의 조건을 정확하게 파악해야 한다. 동일한 규칙이라도 그 조건을 문제에 따라 다소 다르게 설정할 수 있기 때문이다.

b. [함정!] (h)의 'ten cooks'에서 /n/→[ŋ]으로 바뀌지만 뒷소리 /k/와 동일하지 않으므로 total assimilation이라 할 수 없다.

답안

③

과제

⟨B⟩박스에 밑 줄친 단어들을 broad and narrow하게 transcription하세요.

4. 글 〈A〉를 읽고 〈B〉의 밑줄 친 부분에 각각 일어날 수 있는 음운현상을 〈A〉에서 찾아 번호를 쓰시오. (단, 〈A〉에 제시된 조건만을 고려할 것.). 【4 points】 2008-전국17

All languages modify complicated sequences in connected speech in order to simplify the articulation process. The main function of most of the adjustments in English is to promote the regularity of English rhythm – that is, to squeeze syllables between stressed elements and facilitate their articulation so that regular timing can be maintained. Specifically, the following optional phonological processes frequently occur in connected speech in North American English:

(1) Alveolar stops are assimilated in place of articulation to following bilabial or velar stops across word boundaries.
(2) Oral alveolar stops are pronounced as a flap after a stressed vowel and before an unstressed vowel.
(3) Oral alveolar stops are deleted if they are central in a sequence of three consonants.

a. He has a green car.
b. Please send Susan a box of chocolates.
c. Would you care for a bit of cheese?
d. I met Bob yesterday.

출제 영역

Assimilation/Flapping/Deletion

출제 의도

Assimilation/Flapping/Deletion의 음운규칙을 제시하고 해당되는 표현을 찾을 수 있어야 한다. 음운규칙의 조건을 정확하게 파악하는 것이 중요한다.

문제 풀이 과정

A박스 요약 및 핵심내용

(1) Alveolar stops (/t, d, n/) are assimilated in place of articulation to following bilabial (/b, p/) or velar stops (/k, g/) across word boundaries.

(2) Oral alveolar stops (/t, d/) are pronounced as a flap after a stressed vowel and before an unstressed vowel.

(3) Oral alveolar stops (/t, d/) are deleted if they are central in a sequence of three consonants.

B박스 분석 과정

a. He has a green car. 음운현상(1) : /n/+/k/ → [ŋ]+[k]

b. Please send Susan a box of chocolates. 음운현상(3) : /n/+/d/+/s/ → /n/+/s/

c. Would you care for a bit of cheese? 음운현상(2) : /v́/+/t/+/v/ → [-ɾə-]

d. I met Bob yesterday. 음운현상(1) : /t/+/b/ → [b]+[b]

풀이 과정에서 어려운 점

- [주의] Oral stops이란 표현이 들어가면 stops는 oral stops과 nasals를 포함한다.

답안

In the underlined words in (a) and (d), alveolar stops /n, t/ are assimilated to following velar and bilabial sounds, respectively as in (1). In (b), the central alveolar stop /d/ is deleted in a sequence of three consonants as in (3). In (c), the alveolar stop /t/ becomes a flap between a stressed and an unstressed vowel as in (2).

과제

- flapping 현상을 AEP를 참고하여 자세히 정리하세요.
- 자음 세 개가 연속으로 위치할 때 중앙의 자음이 삭제되는 현상을 AEP를 참고하여 자세히 정리하세요.

5. Read the passage and fill in each blank with the ONE most appropriate word. Write your answers in the correct order. 【2 points】 2019-A04

Across morpheme boundaries, obligatory nasal assimilation to bilabials or alveolars applies without restriction, as shown in (1).

(1)	compose	composition
	symbol	symbolic
	sympathy	sympathetic
	condemn	condemnation
	intone	intonation
	indent	indentation

On the other hand, obligatory nasal assimilation to velars applies selectively, as shown in (2). (Note that optional nasal assimilation may apply postlexically to derive 'co[ŋ]cordance,' 'co[ŋ]gressional,' etc.)

(2)	Nasal assimilation	No nasal assimilation
	co[ŋ]cord	co[n]cordance
	co[ŋ]gress	co[n]gressional
	co[ŋ]quer	co[n]cur
	co[ŋ]gruous	co[n]gruity
	sy[ŋ]chrony	sy[n]chronic
	i[ŋ]cubate	i[n]clude

The examples in (2) illustrate that obligatory nasal assimilation applies only when preceded by a(n) ________ vowel and followed by a(n) __________ vowel with a velar involved.

출제 영역

Assimilation

출제 의도

Morpheme boundary에서는 nasal assimilation이 optional 하게 일어나는 경우가 있다. 어떤경우에 일어나고 일어나지 않는지 데이터를 분석하여 환경을 파악할 수 있어야 한다.

문제 풀이 과정

아래 (2)에서 nasal assimilation이 optional 하게 일어난다. 그 환경을 찾아야 한다. 데이터가 'morphologically related words'로 구성되어 있다. 이것은 강세와 관련되어 있다는 것을 의미한다.

(2)

Nasal assimilation	No nasal assimilation
co[ŋ]cord	co[n]cordance
co[ŋ]gress	co[n]gressional
co[ŋ]quer	co[n]cur
co[ŋ]gruous	co[n]gruity
sy[ŋ]chrony	sy[n]chronic
i[ŋ]cubate	i[n]clude

▶ 좌측과 우측이 강세가 다르다. 좌측 단어들은 첫 번째 음절에 강세가 위치하지만 우측 단어들은 두 번째 음절에 강세가 위치한다.

풀이 과정에서 어려운 점

강세 차이라는 점을 찾아야 한다.(힌트는 'morphologically related words'이다.)

답안

stressed, unstressed

과제

문제에 제시된 단어들의 강세 위치를 정확하게 숙지한다.

6. 〈A〉에서 설명하는 음운 현상이 나타나는 문장을 〈B〉에서 3개 찾아 쓰시오. 【3 points】

2007-전국12

> In English we can find a type of assimilation where two segments assimilate to each other. The outcome of this assimilation is a third distinct segment which combines properties of the two assimilating segments. In careful speech, for example, *could you* would be realized as [kʊdjuː]; but in normal conversation it is more likely to be realized as [kʊʤə]. In the example, the alveolar stop [d] and following palatal approximant [j] fuse to give the voiced post-alveolar affricate [ʤ]. The voiced, place, and manner of articulation of the two input segments are combined to form a third segment.

> (In the lobby of a library)
> A: Hi, would you do me a favor?
> B: Yes, what can I do for you?
> A: I think I left my umbrella in the library yesterday.
> B: Oh, did you? Any idea where you left it?
> A: I don't know... But I sat by the window over there.
> B: All right. Just a moment. I'll go and have a look.
> A: Thanks.
> (After some time)
> B: I'm sorry. I couldn't find it anywhere. Why don't you come back tomorrow? I'll ask the janitor if he found it.
> A: Okay, thanks. See you tomorrow.

출제 영역

Assimilation 〉 Coalescence Assimilation 〉 Palatalization

출제 의도

〈A〉에서 Coalescence assimilation현상을 제시하고 그것이 적용된 문장을 〈B〉에서 찾을 수 있어야 한다.

문제 풀이 과정

A박스 요약 및 핵심내용

Coalescence Assimilation 현상: *could you* [kʊdjuː] → [kʊʤə]

B박스 분석 과정

Coalescence Assimilation 현상이 나타나는 문장 3개:

(1) Hi, would you do me a favor?

(2) Oh, did you?

(3) Why don't you come back tomorrow?

풀이 과정에서 어려운 점

[실수] '문장'을 쓰라고 했다. 해당 표현만 쓰면 안된다.

답안

(1) Hi, would you do me a favor?

(2) Oh, did you?

(3) Why don't you come back tomorrow?

과제

1. 위 답안에서 보이는 음운현상의 조건을 쓰고 narrow하게 transcription하세요.
2. 위 답안에서 palatalization이 coalescence가 아닌 regressive assimilation현상으로도 말할 수 있는지 설명해 보세요.

7. Read ⟨A⟩ and ⟨B⟩ and answer the question. 【2 points】 2012-33

> When neighboring sounds mutually affect each other to merge into a third sound, the process is called coalescent assimilation, which can be found in palatalization in English. This coalescent assimilation or palatalization occurs when 'a morpheme-final or word-final alveolar obstruent' is followed by 'the palatal glide' in English, merging the two sounds into 'a palatalized fricative or affricate.' For example, within a word as in *architecture*, the underlying /t/ in the morpheme final position of *architect-* and the initial /j/ in the suffix *-ture* affect each other to merge into the palatalized affricate [ʧ]. This process can also be found across words as in the phrase *kiss you* in fast, casual speech of North American English.

> a. You don't accept your failure easily, do you?
> b. You seem to be under the delusion that he follows you.
> c. The old class divisions had begun to melt down.
> d. We should cut down on our spending next year.
> e. He checked his yacht before his departure for Australia.
> f. After six year, her gracious demeanor became known to everybody.

Which of the following lists all and only sentences that contain the expressions which can undergo the coalescent assimilation described in ⟨A⟩ both within a word and across words?

① a, c, d
② a, d, e
③ b, c, f
④ b, e, f
⑤ c, d, e

출제 영역

Assimilation 〉 Coalescence Assimilation 〉 Palatalization

출제 의도

Coalescence Assimilation의 음운현상을 제시하고 해당 현상이 적용되는 표현을 찾을 수 있어야 한다.

문제 풀이 과정

A박스 요약 및 핵심내용

Coalescent assimilation occurs when 'a morpheme-final or word-final alveolar obstruent' is followed by 'the palatal glide' in English, merging the two sounds into 'a palatalized fricative or affricate.'

e.g., *architecture, kiss you*

B박스 분석 과정

a. You don't <u>accept your</u> failure easily, do you? ▶ within a word
b. You seem to be under the <u>delusion</u> that he <u>follows you</u>. ▶ both within a word and across words
c. The old class <u>divisions</u> had begun to melt down. ▶ within a word
d. We should cut down on our spending <u>next year</u>. ▶ within a word
e. He checked <u>his yacht</u> before his <u>departure</u> for Australia. ▶ both within a word and across words
f. After <u>six year</u>, her <u>gracious</u> demeanor became known to everybody. ▶ both within a word and across words

풀이 과정에서 어려운 점

[함정] 지문에서 'both within a word and across words'과 같이 두 경우가 모두 포함된 문장을 골라야 한다.

답안

④

과제

〈B〉에 palatalization이 적용된 모든 단어 및 표현들은 narrow하게 전사하세요.

8. Read the passage in 〈A〉 and the dialogue in 〈B〉, and follow the directions. 【4 points】
2020-A07

One of the most effective ways of testing a learner's pronunciation is to observe and record repeated errors in a variety of situations. Speech contexts often change the way a given word is pronounced. Careful or emphasized speech is usually employed to show how to pronounce words clearly. In a connected or conversational speech, words are often contracted and the pronunciation of a word can change through the phenomena in (1) and sound rules in (2):

(1) a. That is nice 〉 That's (Contraction)
b. missed *[d], Ms. *[s] (Spelling pronunciation)

(2)

	Careful speech	Connected speech	Sound rules
a. can't you	[tj]	[ʧ]	Palatalization
b. because	[ə]	–	Vowel deletion
c. greater	[t]	[ɾ]	Tapping
d. advantage	[nt]	[n]	Consonant deletion

It is worth mentioning that spelling often influences learners' pronunciation of words. When spelling pronunciation errors are found in learners' pronunciation, they can sometimes be critical. For instance, if the plural form of *sea*, *seas*, is pronounced [sis] rather than [siz], it can be misunderstood as the word *cease* [sis] by listeners.

(Two students are talking about what they wrote during a dictation task without looking at each other's notes.)

S1: Can you tell me what you got for the second sentence? I wrote down, 'Last [wɪnɚ] (winner) was colder,' and it does not make sense to me.

S2: Why? It means what it says. 'Last [wɪntɚ] (winter) was colder.' How (i) did you understand it?

S1: Oh, it is [wɪntɚ] (winter), the season! I thought it was winner. That is why the sentence did not make sense to me.

S2: [wɪntɚ] (winter), [wɪntɚ](winter), ...yes, when you say it quickly, it does sound the same.

S1: Thanks! Wait, did you hear the last word in the fourth sentence? Can you tell me what it was?

S2: 'My dog's skin is irritated by [fliz] (fleas).'

S1: What is [fliz](fleas)? Can you spell it for me?

S2: F-L-E-A-S! Don't you know what fleas are?

S1: Yeah, but isn't that pronounced as (ii) [flis](fleas)?
It is confusing.

S2: Let's ask the teacher later why 's' sounds like 'z' here.

Identify ONE phenomenon or sound rule from 〈A〉 that changes the pronunciation of (i) in 〈B〉 and explain how your answer applies to the given words. Then, identify ONE phenomenon or sound rule that causes S1's confusion in (ii) and explain how your answer applies to the given word based on the description in 〈A〉.

출제 영역

Assimilation 〉 Palatalization

출제 의도

〈A〉에서 제시된 음운현상이 적용된 표현을 알고, 발음의 혼동이 왜 발생하는지 〈A〉에서 찾을 수 있어야 한다.

문제 풀이 과정

A박스 요약 및 핵심내용

In a connected or conversational speech, words are often contracted and the pronunciation of a word can change through the phenomena in (1) and sound rules in (2):

(1) a. That is nice 〉 That's (Contraction)
b. missed *[d], Ms. *[s] (Spelling pronunciation)

(2)

	Careful speech	Connected speech	Sound rules
a. can't you	[tj]	[ʧ]	Palatalization
b. because	[ə]	-	Vowel deletion
c. greater	[t]	[ɾ]	Tapping
d. advantage	[nt]	[n]	Consonant deletion

B박스 분석 과정

(i) did you : palatalization
(ii) [flis](fleas) : spelling pronunciation error

풀이 과정에서 어려운 점

답안

In (i) 'did you', palatalization is involved. The alveolar stop /d/ is palatalized when it is followed by the palatal approximant /j/. In (ii), the spelling pronunciation error is found. S1's pronunciation is influenced by the spelling of the word 'fleas'.

과제

9. Read the passage and follow the directions. 【4 points】 2020-B03

> Some morphemes in English are pronounced differently depending on their phonetic environments. These variants of the same morpheme are called allomorphs. An important question is how we know which allomorph appears for a given word.
>
> Consider the following examples in (1), where the negative morphemes *il*– and *ir*– are added to a base:
>
> (1) a. *il*–: illegal, illogical, illiterate, illegible
>   b. *ir*–: irregular, irrational, irreducible, irrecoverable
>
> Comparing the examples in (1a) with the ones in (1b), a simple distribution is observed for the two allomorphs [ɪl] and [ɪɹ]. That is, [ɪl] and [ɪɹ] are selectively combined with their bases conditioned by the initial sound of the base: when the base begins with /l/, the prefix *il*– is chosen, and when the base begins with /ɹ/, the prefix *ir*– is chosen.
>
> There is another case where [l] and [ɹ] alternate between allomorphs. The adjectival suffix has two allomorphs: –*ar* [əɹ] and –*al*[əl], as shown in (2):
>
> (2) a. –ar: singular, popular, solar, velar
>   b. –al: rural, plural, viral, moral
>
> These suffixes –*ar* [əɹ] and –*al*[əl] are attached to the base depending on the final consonant of the base. (1) and (2) are different in where the morpheme is attached: (1) precedes the base, which is a prefix, and (2) follows the base, which is a suffix. On the other hand, these two morphemes are similar in that the allomorphs for different morphemes show the same alternation between [l] and [ɹ]. It is interesting to find the two apparently different phonemes /l/ and /ɹ/ are involved in the alternation of the allomorphs *il*–/*ir*– and –*al*/–*ar*.
>
> The two sounds /l/ and /ɹ/ share many phonetic properties such as voicing, the place of articulation, and the manner of articulation. They only differ in terms of the way air passes through the mouth. This characteristic difference can be made using the distinctive properties known as the distinctive feature [lateral].

Identify TWO phonological processes involved in (1) and (2) in the correct order. Then, using the distinctive feature [lateral] (i.e., [+lateral] or [−lateral]), generalize the distribution of the allomorphs –al and –ar.

출제 영역

Dissimilation/Assimilation

출제 의도

형태소의 발음 변이(allomorphs)의 환경을 이해하고 그것을 특정 변별자질을 사용하여 기술할 수 있어야 한다. 또한 그 발음변이가 어떤 음운현상과 관련된 것인지 말할 수 있어야 한다.

문제 풀이 과정

1. Allomorphs 현상:

- *'il-'* vs *'ir-'*

(1) a. *il-*: illegal, illogical, illiterate, illegible
b. *ir-*: irregular, irrational, irreducible, irrecoverable

- *'-ar'* vs *'-al'*

(2) a. -ar: singular, popular, solar, velar
b. -al: rural, plural, viral, moral

2. /l/과 /ɹ/의 공통점과 차이점
Voicing, place, manner가 동일하다. 하지만 [lateral]자질에서 차이가 있다.

3. 문제 풀이
a. TWO phonological processes : (1)은 assimilation, (2)는 base마지막 자음이 /l/일때 '-ar'이 붙고 /r/일 때 '-al'이 첨가되므로 dissimilation
b. '-ar'과 '-al' 현상의 일반화 : base 끝에 위치한 자음이 [+lateral]이면 [-lateral]이 포함된 접사를 선택하고 [-lateral]이면 [+laternal]자질의 접사를 선택한다.

풀이 과정에서 어려운 점

- 'TWO phonological processes'를 말하라는 문제는 처음 출제된 유형이라서 잠시 심리적 부담감이 생겼다.
- 관련 용어정리 : allomorphs, morpheme, base, lateral

답안

Assimilation and dissimilation are involved in the data in (1) and (2), respectively. In (2), A suffix that has the [-lateral] feature like '-ar' is attached to the base whose final consonant has the [+lateral] feature, whereas a suffix of the [+lateral] like '-al' is attached to the base whose final consonant has the [-lateral].

과제

주요 phonological processes에 어떤 것들이 있는지 예시와 함께 나열해 보자.

10. Read the description below and follow the directions. 【2 points】 2011-33

> Phonological rules apply to phonemic strings and alter them in various ways to derive their phonetic pronunciations. The underlined part in the following examples from native speakers of English show the application of the rules either diachronically or synchronically.
>
> a. They may add nondistinctive features, which are predictable from the context.
> *Key players on the ski team were sick.*
> b. They may change feature values to make two phonemes in a string more dissimilar.
> *Are there any similar aspects among the spiritual groups?*
> c. They may insert segments that are not present in the phonemic string.
> *The school has many kids from my neighborhood.*
> d. They may delete phonemic segments in a certain context.
> *What's the difference between sign and signature?*

Choose all and only the phonological rules that are shown with correct examples underlined.

① a, b
② a, b, d
③ a, c, d
④ b, c
⑤ c, d

출제 영역

Dissimilation/Deletion/Aspiration

출제 의도

밑줄 친 표현에 적용되는 음운현상을 파악할 수 있어야 하고, 해당 음운현상을 적절하게 정의할 수 있어야 한다.

문제 풀이 과정

다양한 음운현상이 있다:

a. *Key players on the ski team were sick.*

▶ /k/가 aspirated되므로 'They may add nondistinctive features, which are predictable from the context.' 설명은 적절하다.

b. *Are there any similar aspects among the spiritual groups?*

▶ /l/과 /r/의 대비로 인한 이화작용(dissimilation)이다. 따라서 'They may change feature values to make two phonemes in a string more dissimilar.'는 적절한 설명이다.

c. *The school has many kids from my neighborhood.*

▶ Voicing agreement현상이 존재하므로 'They may insert segments that are not present in the phonemic string.'는 부적절하다. 복수형어미 첨가로 인한 insertion현상은 base의 마지막 음이 치찰음(sibilants)일 때만 일어난다.

d. *What's the difference between sign and signature?*

▶ [saɪn]으로 발음되므로 /g/deletion 현상이 일어난다. 'They may delete phonemic segments in a certain context.'설명은 적절하다.

풀이 과정에서 어려운 점

- 해당 밑줄 친 단어에 어떤 음운현상이 적용되는지 알아야 한다.
- 관련용어정리 : diachronically, synchronically, nondistinctive feature,

답안

②

과제

- Aspiration 현상을 AEP를 참고하여 자세히 정리하자.
- dissimilation현상이 일어나는 단어들을 별도로 정리하고 가능 하면 암기하자.
- /g/ deletion현상을 '이동걸전공영어 영어학2'교재를 참고하여 상세히 정리하자.

11. Read the passage and follow the directions. 【4 points】 2017-B03

The schwa vowel /ə/, which is a reduced or weak vowel in English, can be deleted in fast speech, as exemplified in (1).

(1) Schwa Deletion

Careful Speech	Fast Speech
camera ['kæməɹə]	['kæmɹə]
veteran ['vɛtəɹən]	['vɛtɹən]

However, schwa deletion is not observed in fast speed for the following words.

(2) No Schwa Deletion

Careful Speech	Fast Speech	
facilitate [fə'sɪləteɪt]	[fə'sɪləteɪt]	*[fə'sɪlteɪt]
famous ['feɪməs]	['feɪməs]	*['feɪms]

In the following examples of morphologically related words, schwa deletion may or may not be observed.

(3)

	Careful Speech	Fast Speech	
a. principle	['pɹɪnsəpəl]	['pɹɪnspəl]	
principality	[pɹɪnsə'pæləti]	[pɹɪnsə'pæləti]	*[pɹɪns'pæləti]
b. imaginative	[ɪ'mæʤənətɪv]	[ɪ'mæʤnətɪv]	
imagination	[ɪmæʤə'neɪʃən]	[ɪmæʤə'neɪʃən]	*[ɪmæʤ'neɪʃən]

In the data given in (1) and (3), schwa deletion occurs in fast speech under two conditions related to a preceding and a following phonetic environment. State the two phonetic conditions for schwa deletion.

출제 영역

Schwa Deletion

출제 의도

Schwa가 삭제되는 현상을 주어진 Data 분석을 통해 그 환경을 기술할 수 있어야 한다.

문제 풀이 과정

Schwa Deletion 현상

1. Schwa가 삭제될 수 있는 현상과 그렇지 않은 현상 비교:

(1) Schwa Deletion

Careful Speech		Fast Speech	
camera	['kæməɹə]	['kæmɹə]	
veteran	['vɛtəɹən]	['vɛtɹən]	

(2) No Schwa Deletion

Careful Speech		Fast Speech	
facilitate	[fə'sɪləteɪt]	[fə'sɪləteɪt]	*[fə'sɪlteɪt]
famous	['feɪməs]	['feɪməs]	*['feɪms]

Data says :
"다른 schwa가 뒤에 있을 때 앞의 것을 삭제할 수 있지만. 그렇지 않다면 삭제할 수 없어"

2. Morphologically related words에서 schwa가 선택적으로 삭제되는 현상

▶ 'Morphologically related words'라고 언급한 이유는 stress와 관련이 있다는 힌트를 제공하는 것!

(3)

	Careful Speech	Fast Speech	
a. principle	['pɹɪnsəpəl]	['pɹɪnspəl]	
principality	[pɹɪnsə'pæləti]	[pɹɪnsə'pæləti]	*[pɹɪns'pæləti]
b. imaginative	[ɪ'mæʤənətɪv]	[ɪ'mæʤnətɪv]	
imagination	[ɪmæʤə'neɪʃən]	[ɪmæʤə'neɪʃən]	*[ɪmæʤ'neɪʃən]

Data says :
"앞의 모음에 강세가 있을 때는 schwa삭제가 가능하지만 강세가 없을 때는 삭제할 수 없어."

풀이 과정에서 어려운 점

- (1)과 (2)에서 다른 schwa여부가 삭제와 관련이 있다는 것을 찾는것이 어렵다.
- (3)에서는 'Morphologically related words'라는 힌트를 제공했지만 정확하게 data를 분석하는 것이 쉽지 않다.

답안

In English fast speech, a schwa can be deleted when it is preceded by a stressed vowel and followed by another schwa.

과제

- 본문에 제시된 단어의 강세 위치를 정리한다.
- 영어의 리듬에 대해 EPP를 참고하여 정리한다

12. Read the passage and follow the directions. 【5 points】 2015-B03

Words such as *music* [mjuzɪk] and *cube* [kjub] are pronounced in the same way in both American English and British English. However, words such as *tuition*, *endure*, and *annuity* vary, as shown in (1a) and (1b).

(1a) British English

tuition [tjuɪʃən]	duration [djʊreɪʃən]
endure [ɪndjʊə]	annuity [ənjuəti]
perpetuity [pɜːpətjuəti]	voluminous [vəljumənəs]

(1b) American English

tuition [tuɪʃən]	duration [dʊreɪʃən]
endure [ɪndʊə]	annuity [ənuəti]
perpetuity [pɜːpətuəti]	voluminous [vəlumənəs]

While in British English we see a /j/ after the underlined consonants /t/, /d/, /n/, and /l/ in the words given in (la), the expected American English pronunciations are without a /j/ after the same underlined consonants, as shown in (1b). The same difference is observed after the underlined consonants /s/ and /z/ for the words in (2a) and (2b).

(2a) British English

assume [əsjum]	superb [sjupɜːb]
exude [ɪgzjud]	résumé [rɛzjʊmeɪ]

(2b) American English

assume [əsum]	superb [supɜːb]
exude [ɪgzud]	résumé [rɛzʊmeɪ]

However, the words given in (3) show that the underlined alveolars /n/ and /l/ are followed by a /j/ in American English as well as in British English.

(3) British English and American English

continue [kəntɪnju]	biannual [baɪænjuəl]
voluble [vɑljʊbəl]	valuation [væljueɪʃən]

Based on the data given in (1b), (2b), and (3), state the condition(s) when /j/ cannot follow alveolar consonants and the condition(s) when /j/ can in American English.

출제 영역

/j/ dropping

출제 의도

AE에서 /j/가 발음되는 환경과 삭제되는 환경의 차이점을 제시된 data분석을 통해 설명할 수 있어야 한다.

문제 풀이 과정

1. AE와 BrE에서 /j/ 발음 동일
   music [mjuzɪk], *cube* [kjub]

2. AE와 BrE에서 /j/ 발음 차이

(1a) British English

tuition [tjuɪʃən]	duration [djʊreɪʃən]
endure [ɪndjʊə]	annuity [ənjuəti]
perpetuity [pɜːpətjuəti]	voluminous [vəljumənəs]

(2a)

assume [əsjum]	superb [sjupɜːb]
exude [ɪgzjud]	résumé [rɛzjʊmeɪ]

(1b) American English

tuition [tuɪʃən]	duration [dʊreɪʃən]
endure [ɪndʊə]	annuity [ənuəti]
perpetuity [pɜːpətuəti]	voluminous [vəlumənəs]

(2b)

assume [əsum]	superb [supɜːb]
exude [ɪgzud]	résumé [rɛzʊmeɪ]

▶ BrE에서는 /j/를 언제든지 발음하지만, AE는 alveolars /t, d, s, z, n, l/뒤에서 /j/는 발음하지 않는다.

3. /n, l/뒤에서 /j/발음됨

(3) British English and American English

continue [kəntɪnju]	biannual [baɪænjuəl]
voluble [vɑljʊbəl]	valuation [væljueɪʃən]

▶ (1b)와 (2b)에서 /t, d, s, z, n, l/뒤 /j/가 발음되지 않는다고 했다. (3)에서 /n, l/뒤에서 다시 발음된다. (1b)과 (2b)에서 해당 음절이 강세를 갖지만 (3)에서 강세가 없다.

풀이 과정에서 어려운 점

/n, l/뒤에서 /j/가 삭제되는 환경과 발음되는 환경의 차이점을 찾아야 한다.

답안

In American English, /j/ cannot follow an alveolar consonant, whereas /j/ can follow an alveolar sonorant when it is in an unstressed syllable.

과제

13. Read the passage and follow the directions 【4 points】 2006-서울인천11

> Words that contain salient information in a sentence are called content words. They include nouns, verbs, adjectives, and adverbs. The less prominent words in a sentence are called function words. Examples of function words are pronouns, articles, prepositions and conjunctions. In connected speech, function words are pronounced differently than when they are spoken in isolation. Here are some examples:
>
> | Written Form | Spoken Form |
> |---|---|
> | Tom watched her last night. | [ˈtɑm ˈwɑʧt ər ˈlæst ˈnayt] |
> | A cup of tea | [ə ˈkʌp ə ˈtiy] |
> | Give them a break | [ˈgɪv əm ə ˈbreyk] |
> | Now and then | [ˈnaw ən ˈðɛn] |

Consider the examples above and state THREE characteristics of pronunciation of the function words.

출제 영역

Reduction (Deletion)

출제 의도

Function words가 spoken form에서 약화된다. 이 때 약화현상이 구체적으로 어떤 방식으로 일어나는지 기술할 수 있어야 한다.

문제 풀이 과정

1. Content word & Function words
   a. content words : nouns, verbs, adjectives, and adverbs.
   b. function words : pronouns, articles, prepositions and conjunctions.

2. function words의 약화 현상

Written Form	Spoken Form
Tom watched her last night.	['tɑm 'wɑʧt ər 'læst 'nayt]
A cup of tea	[ə 'kʌp ə 'tiy]
Give them a break	['gɪv əm ə 'breyk]
Now and then	['naw ən 'ðɛn]

3. characteristics of pronunciation of the function words.
   'her' /hər/ → [ər] : deletion of a preceding consonant
   'of' /əv/ → [ə] : deletion of a following consonant
   'them' /ðɛm/ → [əm] : deletion of a preceding consonant and vowel reduction
   'and' /ænd/ → [ən] : vowel reduction and deletion of a final consonant

풀이 과정에서 어려운 점

- 제시된 function words의 약화되지 않은 발음을 정확하게 알고 있어야 발음 변화를 말할 수 있다.

답안

First, a word-initial consonant in function words are deleted. Second, a word-final consonant can be deleted. Lastly, the vowel in function words reduces to the schwa.

과제

'AEP'의 4.10 Full forms vs Reduced forms of function words (p.95) 읽고 정리하자.

14. 다음 대화를 읽고, 물음에 답하시오. 【4 points】 2002-전국15

Inho:	Lisa seemed to have much difficulty doing her homework.
James:	Oh, did she? She [maytfθɔ́:t] of asking us for help.
Inho:	Pardon?
James:	I mean I am sorry she didn't think of asking us for help.

a. She _____ _____ ______ of asking us for help.

b. [maytfθɔ́:t]에서 발견되는 음성적 변화 현상 두 가지 기술

출제 영역

Deletion

출제 의도

주어진 표현에 어떤 음운현상이 적용되는지 설명할 수 있어야 한다.

문제 풀이 과정

1. 발음 분석
   [maytfθɔ́:t]는 맥락에 따라 might have thought으로 이해할 수 있다. 이때 might와 thought은 음운현상이 적용되지 않아서 바로 단어를 알 수 있다. 문제는 중간에 [f]가 어떤 단어인지 파악하는것이 핵심이다. 이는 음운현상으로도 알 수 있지만 문법적 지식(가정법)으로도 유추할 수 있다.

2. [maytfθɔ́:t]에서 발견되는 음성적 변화 현상 두 가지 기술
   'have' : [hæv] → [həv] → [əv] → [v] → [f]
   ▶ 이 과정에서 모음약화, /h/삭제, schwa삭제, voicing assimilation 현상이 발생한다.

풀이 과정에서 어려운 점

- 'have'의 다양한 약화 현상을 알아야 한다.

답안

a. might have thought
b. word-initial consonant and schwa deletion in 'have', /v/ becomes /f/ before a voiceless consonant

과제

15. Read the passage in and the examples in , and followthe directions. 【4 points】

2024–B04

⟨A⟩

It is not unusual for a segment to appear repeatedly in a word. However, repeated segments in proximity are sometimes repaired by means of dissimilation, by which a segment becomes less similar to another segment. For example, –al suffix appears in the form of *–ar* to avoid the repetition of /l/ in the final syllable, when it attaches to stems ending with /l/ (e.g., *annual, mental, coronal* vs. *angular, similar, velar*).

Repeated segments are repaired by means of deletion as well as dissimilation. As is well known, most varieties of American English are rhotic, which means /ɹ/ is retained in coda position as in (1).

(1) ranger [ɹeɪnʤəɹ]
curtain [kɜɹtən]
labor [leɪbəɹ]
nursery [nɜɹsəɹi]

But in some of these varieties of American English, word–medial /ɹ/ has been found to be deleted in the following words.

(2) a. corner [kɔnəɹ]
b. farmer [fɑməɹ]
c. Harvard [hɑvəɹd]
d. cursor [kɜsəɹ]

Not only word–medial /ɹ/, but word–final /ɹ/ is also deleted in the varieties. Take a look at the words in (3).

(3) a. terror [tɛɹə]
b. mirror [mɪɹə]
c. bearer [bɛəɹə]
d. fairer [fɛəɹə]

⟨B⟩

a. horror b. corridor c. torture d. proctor

In ⟨B⟩, choose the TWO words in which /ɹ/–deletion can occur as shown in ⟨A⟩. Then state the phonological conditions under which word–medial /ɹ/ is deleted in the varieties.

출제 영역

Deletion /r/

출제 의도

한 단어에 두 segment가 반복될 때 하나를 다른 자질의 단어로 변경하거나 삭제하는 현상을 이해하고, 특히 /r/이 반복될 때 word-medial /ɹ/의 삭제 환경을 data분석을 통해 말할 수 있어야 한다.

문제 풀이 과정

A박스 요약 및 핵심내용

두 segments가 반복될 때

1. Dissimilation

-al suffix appears in the form of -ar to avoid the repetition of /l/ in the final syllable, when it attaches to stems ending with /l/.

(e.g., annual, mental, coronal vs. angular, similar, velar)

2. Deletion

- Deletion of word-medial /ɹ/

In some of these varieties of American English, word-medial /ɹ/ has been found to be deleted in (2)

(1) ranger [ɹeɪndʒəɹ], curtain [kɜɹtən], labor [leɪbəɹ], nursery [nɜɹsəɹi]
(2) corner [kɔnəɹ], farmer [fɑməɹ], Harvard [hɑvəɹd], cursor [kɜsəɹ]

- Deletion of word-final /ɹ/

(3) terror [tɛɹə], mirror [mɪɹə], bearer [bɛəɹə], fairer [fɛəɹə]

B박스 분석 과정

word-medial /ɹ/ deletion이 일어나는 단어를 고르라고 했으니 그 환경을 먼저 파악해야 한다. (1)과 (2)를 살펴보자. (2)에서 word-medial /ɹ/이 삭제되지만 ⟨B⟩의 'corridor'와 'proctor'에서 첫 번째 /r/은 삭제되지 않는다. 이 차이는 음절에서 /r/의 위치이다. (1)에서 삭제 될 수 있는 첫 번째 /r/은 coda 자리에 위치하지만 ⟨B⟩에서 'corridor'/kɔrɪdɔr/와 'proctor'/prɑktər/ 에서 첫 번째 /r/은 모두 onset 자리에 위치한다.

a. horror b. corridor c. torture d. proctor

풀이 과정에서 어려운 점

word-medial /ɹ/의 삭제 환경을 찾는 것이 핵심이다. 삭제 현상의 data는 (1)과 (2)에서 제시하나, 삭제되지않는 현상은 ⟨B⟩에서 찾아야 한다. ⟨B⟩에서 찾아야 한다는 것은 word-medial /ɹ/이 삭제될 수 없는 발음의 단어를 이미 알아야 한다는 것이다.

답안

/ɹ/-deletion can occur in the words: 'horror' and 'torture'. Word-medial /ɹ/ is deleted when it occurs before another /ɹ/ that is in coda position, and it occurs in a postvocalic (coda) position.

과제

16. Read the passage and follow the directions. 【4 points】 2018-B01

> In a number of dialects of British English, a glide is inserted in certain environments, as shown in (1) and (2).
>
> (1) /j/ insertion
>
> | | | |
> |---|---|---|
> | being | /biŋ/ | [bijŋ] |
> | my other (car) | /maɪʌðə/ | [maɪjʌðə] |
> | free a (prisoner) | /friə/ | [frijə] |
> | enjoy ice cream | /ɛnʤɔɪaɪskɹim/ | [ɛnʤɔɪjaɪskɹim] |
>
> (2) /w/ insertion
>
> | | | |
> |---|---|---|
> | sewer | /suə/ | [suwə] |
> | few arrests | /fjuəɹɛsts/ | [fjuwəɹɛsts] |
> | now or never | /naʊənɛvə/ | [naʊwənɛvə] |
> | go away | /goʊəweɪ/ | [goʊwəweɪ] |
>
> However, in such dialect, glide insertion is not attested in the examples in (3). Instead, /ɹ/ is inserted.
>
> (3) No glide insertion
>
> | | | | |
> |---|---|---|---|
> | drawing | [dɹɔɹɪŋ] | *[dɹɔjɪŋ] | *[dɹɔwɪŋ] |
> | ma and pa | [maɹənpa] | *[majənpa] | *[mawənpa] |
> | law and order | [lɔɹənɔdə] | *[lɔjənɔdə] | *[lɔwənɔdə] |
> | media event | [midɪəɹɪvɛnt] | *[midɪəjɪvɛnt] | *[midɪəwɪvɛnt] |

Based on the data given in (1)–(3), provide one single generalization for glide insertion. Then, state the condition(s) for /j/ insertion and the one(s) for /w/ insertion, respectively.

출제 영역

Insertion of Glides

출제 의도

Glides /j, w/가 insertion되는 환경을 데이터분석을 통해 말할 수 있어야 하고, 또한 /j/와 /w/가 삽입되는 환경을 각각 기술할 수 있어야 한다.

문제 풀이 과정

(1) /j/ insertion

being	/biŋ/	[bijŋ]	i _ŋ
my other (car)	/maɪʌðə/	[maɪjʌðə]	aɪ _ʌ
free a (prisoner)	/friə/	[frijə]	i _ə
enjoy ice cream	/ɛndʒɔɪaɪskɹim/	[ɛndʒɔɪjaɪskɹim]	ɔɪ _aɪ

(2) /w/ insertion

sewer	/suə/	[suwə]	u _ə
few arrests	/fjuəɹɛsts/	[fjuwəɹɛsts]	u _ə
now or never	/naʊənɛvə/	[naʊwənɛvə]	aʊ _ə
go away	/goʊəweɪ/	[goʊwəweɪ]	oʊ _ə

(3) No glide insertion

drawing	[dɹɔɹɪŋ]	*[dɹɔjɪŋ]	*[dɹɔwɪŋ]	*ɔ_ɪ
ma and pa	[maɹənpa]	*[majənpa]	*[mawənpa]	*a_ə
law and order	[lɔɹənɔdə]	*[lɔjənɔdə]	*[lɔwənɔdə]	*ɔ_ə
media event	[midɪəɹɪvɛnt]	*[midɪəjɪvɛnt]	*[midɪəwɪvɛnt]	*ə_ɪ

풀이 과정에서 어려운 점

- 환경을 정리한 후 선행하는 모음을 분류할 수 있어야 한다.

답안

The insertion of glides /j/ and /w/ occurs between two vowels where the preceding vowels should be a high vowels or a diphthong ending in a high vowel. The glide /j/ is inserted when the preceding vowel is a high front vowel or a diphthong ending in a high front vowel, whereas the glide /w/ is inserted when the preceding vowel is a high back vowel or a diphthong ending in a high back vowel.

과제

유사한 현상이 'linking /r/' 환경도 AEP를 참고하여 정리하자.

17. Read the passage and follow the directions. 【3 points】 2005-서울인천23

The plural suffix −s is pronounced as [əz] in words like *buses, bushes, benches, mazes, rouges,* and *garages.* These words end with the consonants [s, z, ʃ, ʒ, ʧ, ʤ]. These sounds differ with respect to voicing as well as place and manner of articulation. That is, they do not share any articulatory feature. They do, however, have an auditory property in common: then all have a high-pitched hissing sound quality. The high-pitched hissing sound quality is described by using the feature, *sibilant.* These sounds form the natural class of sibilant consonants in English. Using this feature makes it possible to state a generalization. If we state that [əz] occurs in six different situations, we treat the six consonants as if they were a random collection of sounds with no relation to each other. By referring to the natural class, however, we can state the generalization like this: ______________.

Fill in the bland with about 12 words.

출제 영역

Plural suffix '-s'

출제 의도

Sibilant sounds의 음성학적 특성을 이해하고, plural suffix '-s'가 [əz]로 실현되는 환경을 sibilants를 이용해 설명할 수 있어야 한다.

문제 풀이 과정

• suffix '-s' 의 발음

It is pronounced as [əz]. These words end with the consonants [s, z, ʃ, ʒ, ʧ, ʤ].

buses, bushes, benches, mazes, rouges, and *garages.*

• Property of sibilant

All have a high-pitched hissing sound quality

• Natural class of sibilant

By referring to the natural class, we can state the generalization like this 'the plural suffix '-(e)s' is realized as [əz] when it occurs after a sibilant.

풀이 과정에서 어려운 점

답안

'The plural suffix '-(e)s' is realized as [əz] when it occurs after a sibilant.'

과제

- fricatives vs sibilants vs stridents를 구분하자.

18. Read 〈A〉 and 〈B〉 and follow the directions. 【2 points】 2011-35

We all make speech errors, and they tell us interesting things about language and its use. More than simply amusing, speech errors are linguistically interesting because they provide further evidence for phonological rules and for the decomposition of speech sounds into features. Consider the following speech errors:

	Intended Utterance	Actual Utterance
1.	cup of coffee	cuff of coffee
2.	gave the boy	gave the goy
3.	the zipper is narrow	the nipper is zarrow
4.	gone to seed	god to seen

a. The first error is known as an anticipation error, where a segment that occurs later in a series is repeated in an earlier position. The bilabial stop of the first word *cup* was replaced by a labio-dental fricative of the third word *coffee.*

b. The second error is known as a preservation error, where a segment that occurs earlier in a series is repeated in a later position. The bilabial stop of the third word *boy* was switched with a velar fricative of the first of the first word *gave.*

c. The third error is known as a metathesis error, where two segments switch places. The alveolar fricative of the second word *zipper* and the alveolar nasal of the fourth word *narrow* switched places.

d. In the fourth example, also a metathesis error, the coda consonants of the first and third words were reversed. Hence, the first vowel in the actual utterance lost nasalization because it no longer occurs before a nasal consonant. Instead, the third vowel in the actual utterance is nasalized because it is followed by a nasal consonant.

Choose all and only the statements in 〈B〉 that correctly explain the data in 〈A〉 in terms of phonological rules, and features.

① a, b

② a, c

③ a, c, d

④ b, c, d

⑤ b, d

출제 영역

Metathesis

출제 의도

Speech errors에 대해 이해하고 제시된 data에 대한 설명이 정확하게 설명하는지 판단할 수 있어야 한다.

문제 풀이 과정

A박스 요약 및 핵심내용

- Speech errors 현상과 설명

a. cup of coffee → cuff of coffee

▶ anticipation error: the bilabial stop of the first word *cup* was replaced by a labio-dental fricative of the third word *coffee.*

b. gave the boy → gave the goy

stop으로 수정

▶ preservation error: the bilabial stop of the third word *boy* was switched with a velar fricative of the first of the first word *gave.*

c. the zipper is narrow → the nipper is zarrow

▶ metathesis error: the alveolar fricative of the second word *zipper* and the alveolar nasal of the fourth word *narrow* switched places.

d. gone to seed → god to seen

▶ metathesis error : the first vowel in the actual utterance lost nasalization because it no longer occurs before a nasal consonant. Instead, the third vowel in the actual utterance is nasalized because it is followed by a nasal consonant.

풀이 과정에서 어려운 점

각 현상을 설명한 내용을 꼼꼼하고 정확하게 읽어야 한다. 오답은 오직 단어 하나로 인해 생긴다.

답안

③

과제

speech error는 단어 간에 생길수도 있고 단어 안에서 생길 수도 있다. 그 예를 '이동걸영어학2' 교재를 참고하여 찾아보자.

19. Read 〈A〉 and 〈B〉 and answer the question. 【2.5 points】 2013-30

> A phonological process commonly found in English is neutralization, whereby a phonemic contrast generally observed is not found in a given environment. For example, both /t/ and /d/ are realized as the flap [ɾ] between a stressed and an unstressed vowel in American English, as can be seen in *writer* [ɹaɪɾəɹ] and *rider* [ɹaɪɾəɹ]. By the flapping rule, the phonemic contrast between /t/ and /d/ is lost between a stressed and an unstressed vowel, resulting in the neutralization of the contrast in that position. As another example of neutralization, the vowel /i/ within syllables closed by /ɹ/ (e.g., beer) is produced somewhere between a tense /i/ and a lax vowel /ɪ/ in American English. That is, there is no contrast between a tense and a lax vowel before syllable final /ɹ/, even though this distinction exists elsewhere.

> a. At the beginning of a stressed syllable, an aspirated stop occurs, and an unaspirated stop does not (e.g., pea, tea, key).
> b. In some accent of English, /p, t, k/ in syllable final position are realized as a glottal stop (e.g., tip, pit, kick).
> c. In African American English, /ɪ/ and /ɛ/ are pronounced the same before nasal consonants (e.g., pin, pen)

Which of the following lists all and only the case(s) in 〈B〉 that show(s) the phonological process described in 〈A〉.

① a
② a, b
③ a, b, c
④ b, c
⑤ c

출제 영역

Neutralization

출제 의도

중화 현상을 이해하고 제시된 현상이 중화현상인지 구분할 수 있어야 한다.

문제 풀이 과정

A박스 요약 및 핵심내용

1. Neutralization 현상

   A phonological process commonly found in English is neutralization, whereby a phonemic contrast generally observed is not found in a given environment.

2. Neutralization의 예

   a. flapping : the phonemic contrast between /t/ and /d/ is lost between a stressed and an unstressed vowel *writer* [ɹaɪɾəɹ], *rider* [ɹaɪɾəɹ]

   b. /i/ and /ɪ/ before /r/: there is no contrast between a tense and a lax vowel before syllable final /ɹ/ *beer*

B박스 분석 과정

Neutralization의 예 찾기:

a. At the beginning of a stressed syllable, an aspirated stop occurs, and an unaspirated stop does not (e.g., pea, tea, key).

▶ /p, t, k/가 모두 aspirated된다고 해서 변별성이 사라지지 않는다. 각 음이 서로 다른 음소의 이음들이기 때문이다.

b. In some accent of English, /p, t, k/ in syllable final position are realized as a glottal stop (e.g., tip, pit, kick).

▶ /p, t, k/가 모두 glottal stop [ʔ]으로 발음되면 가 음소의 contrastiver가 사라진다. 따라서 중화현상이다.

c. In African American English, /ɪ/ and /ɛ/ are pronounced the same before nasal consonants (e.g., pin, pen)

▶ /ɪ/ and /ɛ/가 영어에서 음소인데 nasals앞에서 동일하게 발음된다면 contrastive가 사라진다. 중화현상에 속한다.

풀이 과정에서 어려운 점

중화현상(neutralization)을 알고 있다면 쉽게 풀 수 있다.

답안

④

과제

중화현상이 다소 혼동될 수 있다. AEP를 참고하여 다양한 중화현상의 예를 찾아보고 정리하자.

20. Read the passage and follow the directions. 【4 points】 2014-A05

There are two types of derivational suffix *−al*: the type that attaches to nouns and forms adjectives as in *central, coastal,* and *musical,* and the type that attaches to verbs and forms noun as in *refusal, proposal,* and *recital.* The second type, called a deverbal suffix, can derive well-formed nouns only if three requirements are satisfied. One is that the final syllable of the verb it attaches to has stress, and based on this requirement, English lacks nouns like **fidgetal, *promisal,* and **abandonal.* The data in (1) and (2) exemplify the other two requirements.

Requirement 2:

(1) betrothal, arrival, acquittal
*rebukal, *impeachal, *detachal

Requirement 3:

(2) rental, dispersal, rehearsal
*acceptal, *resistal, *engraftal

Some Distinctive Features for Consonants

Distinctive Features	Labials	Dentals/ Alveolars	Palato-alveolars	Velar
[anterior]	+	+	−	−
[coronal]	−	+	+	−

Distinctive Features	Nasal stops	Oral stops	Fricatives	Liquids/ Glides
[sonorant]	+	−	−	+
[continuant]	−	−	+	+

Describe Requirements 2 and 3 based on the data in (1) and (2), respectively. For each requirement, use ONE or TWO distinctive features from the list above.

출제 영역

Suffixes

출제 의도

Noun forming Suffix '-al'이 동사에 첨가되는 조건을 주어진 데이터 분석을 통해 말할 수 있어야 한다. 특히 '-al'첨가 조건에 distinctive features을 사용할 수 있어야 한다.

문제 풀이 과정

1. Two types of derivational suffix *-al*:
   a. the type that attaches to nouns and forms adjectives : *central, coastal, musical*
   b. the type that attaches to verbs and forms noun : *refusal, proposal, recital.*

2. The second type (deverbal suffix) 조건:

• Requirement 1: **fidgetal, *promisal,* and **abandonal*

▶ The final syllable of the verb it attaches to has stress

• Requirement 2: betrothal, arrival, acquittal
*rebukal, *impeachal, *detachal

▶ /θ, v, t/ (labials, alveolars) vs. */k, ʧ/ (palato-alveoalr, velar) : [+anterior] vs [-anterior]

• Requirement 3: rental, dispersal, rehearsal
*acceptal, *resistal, *engraftal

▶ -al앞 자음을 선행하는 자음 분류: /n, r/ vs. /p, s, f/ → [+sonorant] vs [-sonorant]

풀이 과정에서 어려운 점

- 분류된 자음을 변별자질로 표현해야 한다

답안

Requirement 2 is that the deverbal suffix '-al' can be attached to a verb whose word final consonant has [+anterior] feature. Requirement 3 is that the suffix '-al' can be attached to a verb whose final consonant has [+anterior] feature immediately preceded by a [+sonorant] consonant.

과제

- 주요 변별자질에 대해 '이동걸영어학2' 교재를 참고하여 정리한다.

21. Read the passage in ⟨A⟩ and ⟨B⟩, and follow the directions. 【4 points】 2023-B04

Many derivational suffixes in English share the same phonological forms, but serve different morphological functions. One example of this is the derivational suffix *−al*. Consider the following words ending in *−al* in (1). Some *−al* words are adjectives and others are nouns.

(1)

−al adjectives	*−al* nouns
annual	dismissal
natural	betrayal
gradual	reversal
federal	survival
floral	renewal
legal	referral

The noun-forming suffix *−al* imposes a morphological and a phonological requirement on the stems to which it attaches. From the morphological perspective, the noun-forming suffix *−al* must attach to a verb, as shown in *dismiss+al*, *betray+al*, *reverse+al*, etc. Not all verbs, however, can take the noun-forming suffix *−al*. Impossible *−al* nouns are shown in (2).

(2) *abandonal *fidgetal *investigatal *promisal *qualifial

English verbs and nouns exhibit a wide range of stress patterns. These are represented by the ultimate, penultimate, or antipenultimate stress, or by the trochaic or iambic foot structure, etc. The phonological requirement, in relation to stress and foot structure, for the noun-forming suffix *−al* can explain why the suffix sometimes creates unattested nouns. The attested *−al* nouns in (1) and the unattested ones in (2) differ markedly in their stress and foot patterns. The stress pattern shared in common among the attested *−al* nouns is also found in many underived nouns, as illustrated in (3).

(3) appendix Chicago veranda avocado
consensus hiatus Minnesota arena

Note: '*' indicates an unattested word.

The above data show that both attested *−al* nouns in (1) and underived nouns in (3) have the primary stress on the ①________ syllable, creating a(n) ____②____ foot at the end.

Fill in the blanks 1 and 2 in ⟨B⟩ each with ONE word from ⟨A⟩, in the correct order. Then, state the phonological generalization that determines which verb stem the noun-forming suffix −al can attach to.

출제 영역

Suffix '-al'

출제 의도

Suffix '-al'가 동사에 첨가될 때 음운조건을 강세위치와 음보구조로 말할 수 있어야 한다.

문제 풀이 과정

A박스 요약 및 핵심내용

Noun-forming suffix -*al*의 첨가 조건

1. Morphological requirement : the noun-forming suffix -*al* must attach to a verb

    dismiss+al, betray+al, reverse+al

★2. Phonological requirement : stress and foot structure

The attested -*al* nouns in (1) and the unattested ones in (2) differ markedly in their stress and foot patterns.

(1) dismissal, betrayal, reversal, survival, renewal, referral

(2) *abandonal *fidgetal *investigatal *promisal *qualifial

3. Underived Noun과 the attested -al nouns의 공통적인 stress patterns

▶ 위 Phonological requirement의 대한 hint 제공

(3) a{ppéndix} Chi{cágo} ve{ránda} avo{cádo}
con{sénsus} hi{átus} Minne{sóta} a{réna}

B박스 분석 과정

▶ 지문의 'These are represented by the ultimate, penultimate, or antipenultimate stress, or by the trochaic or iambic foot structure, etc.' 내용을 참고로 빈칸 답안과 서술형 답안을 작성하면 된다.

1. 'The above data show that both attested -*al* nouns in (1) and underived nouns in (3) have the primary stress on the ①________ syllable, creating a(n) ②________ foot at the end.'

    ▶ (1)과 (3)의 강세는 penultimate syllable에 위치하고 foot구조는 뒤를 기준으로 trochaic foot구조이다.

2. the phonological generalization that determines which verb stem the noun-forming suffix -*al* can attach to:

    dismîss+al, betráy+al, revérs+al, survív+al, renéw+al, reférr+al

▶ '-al'이 첨가되는 동사의 강세는 ult에 위치하고 iambic(약강격) foot구조를 갖는다.

풀이 과정에서 어려운 점

- 지문 전체를 읽으면서 문제의 출제의도를 이해하기 어려움
- 일반적으로 영어는 trochaic구조를 갖지만 이 문제에는 trochaic/iambic 두 개 유형을 제시하고, 이들 구조의 정의를 명시적으로 제시하지 않았다.

답안

penultimate, trochaic

The noun-forming suffix '-al' can attach to verb stems that have the primary stress on the ultimate syllable and the iambic foot structure.

과제

- Trochaic과 iambic foot 구조를 정리하고 이해해야 한다.

22. Read the passage in and the examples in , and followthe directions. 【4 points】

2025-B06

〈A〉

Many inflectional affixes in English are sensitive to phonological properties of base words that they attach to. One example is the comparative affix *-er* that attaches to adjectivesas follows:

(1)

Base adjectives	Suffixed comparatives
smart	smarter
intelligent	*intelligenter
pretty	prettier
attractive	*attractiver

It appears that the attested base adjectives in (1) are no longer than two syllables. Consider the following words in (2), in which the comparative affix *-er* attaches to disyllabic adjectives.

(2)

Base adjectives	Suffixed comparatives
happy	happier
tiny	tinier
brainy	brainier
mighty	mightier

While the affix *-er* attaches to various adjectives, the words in (3) indicate that not all disyllabic adjectives can take the affix *-er*.

(3)

Base adjectives	Suffixed comparatives
afraid	*afraider
naked	*nakeder
active	*activer
verdant	*verdanter

Note: '*' indicates unattested comparatives.

〈B〉

a. avid b. fancy c. jealous d. narrow

Based on 〈A〉, choose the TWO adjectives in which the comparative affix -er can attach to. Then, based on 〈B〉 and, state the phonological conditions for the attested and unattested disyllabic adjectives, respectively.

출제 영역

Suffix '-er'

출제 의도

Suffix '-er'이 첨가되는 base의 조건을 data분석을 통해 설명하고, 더불어 -er 첨가가 가능한 형용사도 구분할 수 있어야 한다.

문제 풀이 과정

A박스 요약 및 핵심내용

Inflectional affixes '-er'이 첨가 조건

1. 음절 수 제한 :It appears that the attested base adjectives in (1) are no longer than two syllables.

(1)

Base adjectives	Suffixed comparatives
smart	smarter
intelligent	*intelligenter
pretty	prettier
attractive	*attractiver

2. 추가 조건?

The comparative affix -er attaches to disyllabic adjectives.

(2)

Base adjectives	Suffixed comparatives
happy	happier
tiny	tinier
brainy	brainier
mighty	mightier

Not all disyllabic adjectives can take the affix -er.

(3)

Base adjectives	Suffixed comparatives
afraid	*afraider
naked	*nakeder
active	*activer
verdant	*verdanter

▶ suffix가 첨가되는 조건 중 가장 중요하게 고려해야 하는 점은 접사와 바로 가까이 위치하는 base의 segment이다. (2)는 base의 마지막 segment가 vowel이고 (3)은 consonant이다.

B박스 분석 과정

a. avid - consonant
b. fancy - vowel → -er 첨가 불가능
c. jealous - vowel → -er 첨가 불가능
d. narrow - consonant

풀이 과정에서 어려운 점

- '-er'이 첨가되는 형용사 마지막 segment를 정확하게 vowel vs consonant로 분류할 수 있어야 한다.

답안

The comparative affix *-er* can attach to adjectives like (b) and (d). Attested disyllabic adjectives typically end in a vowel, whereas unattested ones tend to end in a consonant.

과제

Suffix가 첨가되는 조건의 문제를 보면서 첨가 조건의 주로 무엇인지 분석해 본다.

CHAPTER

04

Syllable

세부영역		출제년도	내용
1. Syllables	1.1 Syllable Structure	2014-A11	Velarized /l/ (rhyme)
		2016-A05	Rhyme
	1.2 Sonority	2013-29	Sonority
	1.3 Phonotactics	2018-A04 2022-A04 2023-A06	Stress patterns Coronal Sounds Sonority Sequencing Principle

❑ 연도별 출제빈도

2002	2003	2004	2005	2006	2007	2008	2009	2010	2011	2012	2013	2014	2015	2016	2017	2018	2019	2020	2021	2022	2023	2024	2025	2026
											*	*		*		*				*	*			?

1. Read the passage and fill in the blank with ONE word. 【2 points】 2014-A11

> In English, the lateral phoneme /l/ has two allophones: 'clear l', [l], and 'dark l', [ɫ], a velarized alveolar lateral. The articulatory difference between the two is that in the former the back of the tongue is lowered while in the latter it is raised toward the velum or retracted toward the uvula (without making contact in either case). Some examples with [l] and [ɫ] are:
>
> (1) limb [lɪm], climb [klaɪm], lock [lɑk]
> (2) miller [mɪlər], yellow [jɛlou], billow [bɪbou]
> (3) mill [mɪɫ], fill [fɪɫ], pile [paɪɫ]], milk [mɪɫk]
> (4) middle [mɪdɫ̩], bubble [bʌbɫ̩], tunnel [tʌnɫ̩]
>
> We can see that [l] and [ɫ] are in complementary distribution. [l] appears in an onset position as in (1) and (2). while [ɫ] appears in a coda position as in (3). The rule involved seems to be that velarization takes place whenever /l/ is in a coda position. However, the cases in (4) cannot be explained by this rule because [ɫ] is syllabic and constitutes the nucleus, which is usually occupied by a vowel. By minimally modifying the above rule, we can obtain a more accurate rule /l/ is velarized if and only if it is part of the ________ .

출제 영역

Syllable & velarized [l]

출제 의도

/l/의 두 이음의 환경을 이해하고 주어진 데이터를 통해 velarized /l/의 환경을 정교화 할 수 있어야 한다.

문제 풀이 과정

1. two allophones : 'clear l', [l], and 'dark l', [ɫ]

(1) limb [lɪm], climb [klaɪm], lock [lɑk]
(2) miller [mɪlər], yellow [jɛlou], billow [bɪbou]
(3) mill [mɪɫ], fill [fɪɫ], pile [paɪɫ]], milk [mɪɫk]
(4) middle [mɪdɫ], bubble [bʌbɫ], tunnel [tʌnɫ]

2. clear l', [l], and 'dark l', [ɫ] 분포
[l] and [ɫ] are in complementary distribution: [l] in an onset position as in (1) and (2), [ɫ] in a coda position as in (3).

3. [ɫ]의 환경 정교화
In (4), /l/ is velarized if and only if it is part of the rhyme. ((4)에서 [ɫ]이 syllabic이므로 nucleus 위치한다.) ▶ (3) coda + (4) nucleus = rhyme

풀이 과정에서 어려운 점

Syllabic /l/의 nucleus position에 위치한다는 점과 coda와 nucleus가 rhyme의 구성요소라는 것을 알아야한다.

답안

rhyme

과제

2. Read the passage and fill in the blank with a distinctive feature. 【2 points】 2016-A05

> In the syllable structure of English words, dependencies between peaks and codas provide evidence for the existence of rhyme as a constituent of syllable. For example, we can see the relationship /aʊ/ peak and its coda as follows:
>
> | | | | | |
> |---|---|---|---|---|
> | (1) | town | [taʊn] | (2) | *[taʊm]/*[taʊŋ] |
> | | house | [haʊs] | | *[haʊf] |
> | | rouse | [raʊz] | | *[raʊv]/*[raʊg] |
> | | sprout | [spraʊt] | | *[spraʊp]/*[spraʊk] |
> | | loud | [laʊd] | | *[laʊb]/*[laʊg] |
> | | mouth | [maʊθ] | | *[maʊf] |
> | | couch | [kaʊʧ] | | *[kaʊg] |
>
> The examples in (1) show that the coda following /aʊ/ has to be ________, while those in (2) show that it cannot be [labial] or [dorsal] to form a rhyme.
>
> *Note*: * indicates a non-permissible form.

출제 영역

Syllable & Coronal feature

출제 의도

음절에서 nucleus와 coda는 rhyme의 성분이다. 즉, nucleus와 coda가 하나의 단위라는 의미는 서로 밀접한 관계를 갖는다는 것을 말한다. 주어진 데이터를 분석하여 /aʊ/와 함께하는 coda가 어떤 자음들인지 분석할 수 있어야 한다.

문제 풀이 과정

- 음절의 peaks과 codas 위치의 관계

Relationship /aʊ/ peak and its coda:

					/aʊ/환경	
(1)	town	[taʊn]	(2)	*[taʊm]/*[taʊŋ]	t_n	*t_m/ŋ
	house	[haʊs]		*[haʊf]	h_s	*h_f
	rouse	[raʊz]		*[raʊv]/*[raʊg]	r_z	*r_v/g
	sprout	[spraʊt]		*[spraʊp]/*[spraʊk]	r_t	*r_p/k
	loud	[laʊd]		*[laʊb]/*[laʊg]	l_d	*l_b/g
	mouth	[maʊθ]		*[maʊf]	m_θ	*m_f
	couch	[kaʊʧ]		*[kaʊg]	k_ʧ	*k_g

▶ 주변소리를 분석하면 /aʊ/뒤에 위치한 자음이 그 원인이라는 것을 알 수 있다. 즉, /aʊ/는 coda에 /n, s, z, t, d, θ, ʧ/를 허용하고 /m, f, v, p, b/와 /ŋ, g, k/는 허용하지 않는다.

- /n, s, z, t, d, θ, ʧ/ : [coronal]
- /m, f, v, p, b/ : [labial]
- /ŋ, g, k/ : [dorsal]

풀이 과정에서 어려운 점

/n, s, z, t, d, θ, ʧ/이 [coronal]자질을 공유하는 자음이라는 것을 파악해야 한다.

답안

[coronal]

과제

- place of articulation에 해당하는 주요 distinctive features들을 나열하고 정의하세요.

3. Read 〈A〉 and 〈B〉 and answer the question. 【2 points】 2013-29

Although nearly everybody can identify individual syllables, it is difficult to define what is meant by a syllable. One possible theory of the syllable draws on the concept of sonority. The sonority of a sound is its loudness relative to that of other sounds with the same length, stress, and pitch. It is generally agreed that the sonority hierarchy is as follows:

less sonorous ←——————————→ more sonorous

stop   fricatives   nasals   liquids   glides   vowels

The sonority theory of the syllable holds that a peak of sonority defines a syllable. That is, according to the theory, the peak of a syllable coincides with the peak of sonority. For example, in a sequence of sounds, [sænd], the vowel is more sonorous than [s] and [n], and [n] is more sonorous than [d]. This sequence of sounds forms one sonority peak on the vowel. Therefore, the theory correctly predicts that this word has one syllable.

a. bright   b. speed   c. dance   d. sweet

Which of the following lists all and only the examples in 〈B〉 that support the theory described in 〈A〉?

① a, b, c
② a, c, d
③ b, c, d
④ b, d
⑤ c, d

출제 영역

Syllable

출제 의도

음절을 a peak of sonority으로 정의하고 그 정의에 맞는 예를 찾을 수 있어야 한다.

문제 풀이 과정

A박스 요약 및 핵심내용

- Syllable의 정의 : a peak of sonority defines a syllable

  sonority hierarchy : stop 〈 fricatives 〈 nasals 〈 liquids 〈 glides 〈 vowels

B박스 분석 과정

- 위 정의에 맞는 예? a, c, d가 위 이론에 적합함
  - a. bright /braɪt/ : stop+liquids+vowel+stop → 1 peak, 1 syllable
  - b. speed /spid/ : fricative+stop+vowel+stop → 2 peak, 1 syllable
  - c. dance /dæns/ : stop+vowel+nasal+fricative → 1 peak, 1 syllable
  - d. sweet /swit/ : fricative+glide+vowel+stop → 1 peak, 1 syllable

풀이 과정에서 어려운 점

답안

②

과제

음절(syllable)의 정의와 분절(syllabification) 방법을 AEP를 참고하여 정리하자.

4. Read the passage and follow the directions. 【2 pints】 2018-A04

It is well known in English that we get antepenultimate stress in nouns of at least three syllables when the penultimate syllable is light:

(1) antepenultimate syllable stressed
cinema, asterisk, America, Canada, animal

When the penultimate syllable ends with a coda, or has a long vowel or a diphthong, stress, however, falls on that heavy penultimate syllables:

(2) penultimate syllable stressed
a. *utensil, agenda, synopsis*
b. *aroma, horizon, arena*

In the above examples in (2a), it is clear that a syllable boundary seats itself between word-internal consonantal sequences such as -ns- (in *utensil*), -nd- (in *agenda*), and -ps- (in *synopsis*), since English phonotactic constraint does not permit such consonantal sequences to occur as an onset cluster. However, the word-internal consonantal sequence -st- poses an interesting challenge for syllabification. Unlike the -ns-, -nd-, or -ps-, the -st- sequence could be an onset cluster (as in *student, stupid*) or a coda cluster (as in *list, mist*).

Fill in the blank with the ONE most appropriate word from the passage above.

Considering the stress placement in the words given in (3) where -st- occurs, we can claim that the underlined s is in ______ position.

(3) antepenultimate syllable stressed
amnesty, minister, pedestal

출제 영역

Stress & Phonotactics

출제 의도

강세받는 음절은 heavy해야한다. 만약 light하다면 강세를 받을 수 없다. 해당 음절이 heavy한지 light한지 알아야 하고, 더불어 phonotactic constraint를 이해해야 한다.

문제 풀이 과정

A박스 요약 및 핵심내용

1. Noun 강세 패턴

Antepenultimate stress when the penultimate syllable is light in (1); penultimate stress when it is heavy in (2):

(1) antepenultimate syllable stressed
cinema, asterisk, America, Canada, animal

(2) penultimate syllable stressed
a. *utensil, agenda, synopsis*
b. *aroma, horizon, arena*

2. Syllable boundary : Unlike the -ns-, -nd-, or -ps-, the -st- sequence could be an onset cluster (as in *student, stupid*) or a coda cluster (as in *list, mist*).

B박스 분석 과정

▶ Noun은 penultimate syllable이 heavy하다면 그 위치에 강세가 일반적으로 위치한다. 하지만 그 음절이 light하다면 강세는 앞 음절에 위치한다. 따라서 penult가 heavy한지 light한지 정확하게 판단해야한다. 그러기 위해서는 영어의 phonotactic constraint를 이해해야 한다. 'st'는 onset과 coda의 cluster로 모두 가능하다. 만약 'st'가 모음사이에 위치한다면 maximal onset principle에 의해 onset에 위치해야 한다. 이러한 원리에 따르면 penult는 light하여 강세가 위치할 수 없다.

(3) antepenultimate syllable stressed
amnesty, minister, pedestal

풀이 과정에서 어려운 점

- 문제의 내용은 전체적으로 좋으나 답안을 찾는 건 매우 쉽다.
- 용어정리 : antepenultimate, penultimate, phonotactics

답안

onset

과제

- Noun과 adjective의 강세 패턴을 AEP를 참고하여 정리한다.
- Verb의 강세 패턴을 AEP를 참고하여 정리한다.
- 영어의 음소배열규칙(phonotactics)를 AEP를 참고하여 정리한다.
- maximal onset principle의 개념을 정리한다.
- 음절의 heavy/light의 개념을 정리한다.

5. Read the passage and follow the directions. 【2points】 2022-A04

When two consonants appear word-initially, the sonority of the first consonant is lower than that of the second one except for '/s/ and voiceless obstruent' sequences such as [st] in *stop* and [sf] in *sphere*. Accordingly, the two liquids /l/ and /ɹ/ appear as the second consonant since they have relatively high sonority. However, it is not the case that all the combinations are possible as below.

[pl]	[bl]	[fl]	[kl]	[gl]
play	*bleed*	*fly*	*click*	*glass*
[pɹ]	[bɹ]	[fɹ]	[kɹ]	[gɹ]
pray	*breed*	*fry*	*crick*	*grass*
*[θl]	*[tl]	*[dl]	[sl]	*[ʃl]
----	----	----	slide	----
[θɹ]	[tɹ]	[dɹ]	*[sɹ]	[ʃɹ]
thrive	*try*	*dry*	----	*shrimp*

As presented above, some consonant clusters including a liquid as the second do not appear in word-initial positions except for a few loanwords. As a result, the contrast between the two liquids /l/ and /ɹ/ is neutralized after ________ obstruents in word-initial positions.

Note: ' * ' indicates a non-permissible form.

출제 영역

Syllable and Phonotactics

출제 의도

음소배열규칙의 기본원리를 이해하고 제시된 자음들을 적절하게 분류할 수 있어야 한다.

문제 풀이 과정

A박스 요약 및 핵심내용

1. 영어의 phonotactics 원리

When two consonants appear word-initially, the sonority of the first consonant is lower than that of the second one except for '/s/ and voiceless obstruent' sequences such as [st] in *stop* and [sf] in *sphere*.

2. 구체적인 phonotactic constraint 실예

[pl]	[bl]	[fl]	[kl]	[gl]	/p, b, f, k, g/는 두 liquids /l/, /r/과 함께 onset cluster로 허용된다.
play	*bleed*	*fly*	*click*	*glass*	
[pɹ]	[bɹ]	[fɹ]	[kɹ]	[gɹ]	
pray	*breed*	*fry*	*crick*	*grass*	

*[θl]	*[tl]	*[dl]	[sl]	*[ʃl]	/θ, t, d, s, ʃ/는 두 liquids중 하나만 onset cluster로 허용된다.
----	----	----	slide	----	
[θɹ]	[tɹ]	[dɹ]	*[sɹ]	[ʃɹ]	
thrive	*try*	*dry*	----	*shrimp*	

3. 문제 이해

▶ 위쪽 데이터는 두 liquids와 모두 사용되는 예이다. 즉, /l/과 /r/는 contrastive하게 사용된다고 말할 수 있다. 하지만 아래쪽 데이터는 둘 중 하나만 사용되므로 'neutralized'하다라고 말할 수 있다.

풀이 과정에서 어려운 점

- 빈칸이 포함된 문장의 표현이 다소 이해하기 어렵다. 일반적으로 사용되는 neutralize의미가 확장되어 사용되었기 때문이다. (수험자의 순발력이 필요한 부분이다.)
- 주어진 data를 읽어내기가 쉽지 않다.
- /p, b, f, k g/와 /θ, t, d, s, ʃ/를 구분할 수 있어야 한다.

답안

coronal

과제

- SSP (sonority scale principle)에 대해 이해하자.
- 용어정리 : labials, dorsals, coronals

6. Read the passage in ⟨A⟩ and the examples in ⟨B⟩, and follow the directions. 【4 points】

2023-A06

Native speakers' intuitions about possible and impossible words are heavily influenced by the phonological properties of sound sequences, represented by relative differences in sonority, i.e., how resonant one sound is compared to the other.

A group of English native speakers were asked to decide how each of the following nonsense words sounds to them, and to give each word a numerical rating, from '1' to '5', according to how confident the respondents are that those are English-like words. '1' meant that the word is definitely not English-like, and '5' meant that it can definitely be an English word. Their averaged ratings for the words are shown in (1).

(1)

Words	Mean scores
bod [bad]	4.66
timp [timp]	4.30
rog [rog]	4.20
mbotto [mbato]	1.07

It appears that native speakers of English perceive words with simple onset to be more English-like than those with complex onset, and simply reject words that violate the phonotactics in English. However, the presence of onset clusters and legitimate phonotactics do not fully explain how the speakers' intuitions work. Another group of English native speakers were asked to do the same task for a different set of nonsense words, as illustrated in (2).

(2)

Words	Mean scores
shliz [ʃliz]	4.16
zloog [zlug]	3.76
nfape [nfeip]	1.98
mvupe [mvup]	1.76

a. kneeb [knib]　　b. rviss [rvis]

c. znape [zneɪp]　　d. nkob [nkob]

Based on ⟨A⟩, first, identify the TWO nonsense words in ⟨B⟩ that are likely to result in a low rating (closer to '1'). Then, state the ONE phonological generalization that can explain both why *bod*, *timp*, and *rog* are considered more English-like than *mbotto* in (1) and why *shliz* and *zloog* are considered more English-like than *nfape* and *mvupe* in (2).

출제 영역

Syllable 〉 Phonotactics

출제 의도

영어에서 음소배열규칙(phonotactics)이 적용될 때 Segments의 공명성(sonority)이 중요한 역할을 한다는 점을 이해하고 적용할 수 있어야 한다.

문제 풀이 과정

A박스 요약 및 핵심내용

Phonotactics

- Simple onset vs. Complex onset / phonotactics

(1)

Words	Mean scores
bod [bad]	4.66
timp [timp]	4.30
rog [rog]	4.20
mbotto [mbato]	1.07

- What judgement?

▶ SSP(sonority scale principle)이 판단 근거가 된다. onset cluster는 sonority가 증가해야하고, coda cluster는 감소해야 한다.

(2)

Words	Mean scores
shliz [ʃliz]	4.16
zloog [zlug]	3.76
nfape [nfeip]	1.98
mvupe [mvup]	1.76

B박스 분석 과정

a. kneeb [knib] → stop+nasal : sonority 증가
b. rviss [rvis] → liquid+fricative : sonority 감소 (SSP위반)
c. znape [zneɪp] → fricative+nasal : sonority 증가
d. nkob [nkob] → nasal+stop : sonority 감소 (SSP위반)

풀이 과정에서 어려운 점

- (2)의 데이터가 무엇을 말하고자 하는지 잘 파악해야 한다.

답안

The words in (b) and (d) are the nonsense words. Within a syllable, the sonority increases as it approaches the nucleus and decreases as it moves toward the margins.

과제

- 영어의 자음과 모음의 sonority를 AEP를 참고하여 정리하자.
- SSP의 개념을 정리하자.

CHAPTER

05

Stress

세부영역		출제년도	내용
1. Stress	1.1 Word stress	2007-서울인천17	Heavy Rhyme
		2008-전국14	Three syllable verbs/nouns
		2025-B04	Name game
	1.2 Stress and suffix	2016-A06	Adjective suffix *-y*
	1.3 Stress Shift	2024-A06	Rhythm reversal
		2010-33	Stress-shifting suffix

❑ 연도별 출제빈도

2002	2003	2004	2005	2006	2007	2008	2009	2010	2011	2012	2013	2014	2015	2016	2017	2018	2019	2020	2021	2022	2023	2024	2025	2026
					*	*		*						*								*	*	?

1. Read the passage and fill in each blank using phrases from it. 【3 points】 2007-서울인천17

English has a set of principles or rules which allow native speakers to assign stress to the appropriate syllable of a word. The unit of a syllable may contain as its core a long vowel or a short vowel, a monophthong or a diphthong, or one or multiple consonants before or after the core.

Consider the following two-syllable verbs:

ballot	exclude	attract	annoy	divide
abstract	enter	delight	incline	salute
contain	feature	protest	portion	signal

We can see that the stress may fall on either the first or the second syllable. Since stress placement rules usually apply to the final syllable first, compare the underlined rhyme sections of the stressed second syllables with the rhymes of the unstressed counterparts. We notice that the final syllable is stressed when it contains (1)_______, (2)_______, or (3)_______ in its rhyme section. That is, the final syllable is stressed when its rhyme is "heavy" in a sense.

출제 영역

Stress & Stressed syllable

출제 의도

강세를 받을 수 있는 음절의 rhyme은 heavy해야 한다. heavy와 light의 개념을 정확하게 이해해야 하고 제시된 단어의 강세위치와 발음을 알고 있어야 문제에 접근할 수 있다.

문제 풀이 과정

1. 영어의 강세 할당 원리 : heavy and light
2. 동사의 강세 패턴 : Stress placement rules usually apply to the final syllable first,
3. 데이터 분석 : compare the underlined rhyme sections of the stressed second syllables with the rhymes of the unstressed counterparts

ballot	exclude	attract	annoy	divide
abstract	enter	delight	incline	salute
contain	feature	protest	portion	signal

a. stressed second syllables

exclude	/−klud/
attract	/−trækt/
annoy	/−nɔɪ/
divide	/−vaɪd/
abstract	/−trækt/
delight	/−laɪt/
incline	/−klaɪn/
salute	/−lut/
contain	/−teɪn/
protest	/−test/

b. unstressed second syllables

ballot	/−lət/
enter	/−tər/
feature	/−ʧər/
portion	/−ʃən/
signal	/−nəl/

▶ Stressed second syllabled의 rhyme의 구성은 a long vowel and one or multiple consonants after the core, a short vowel and multiple consonants after the core, a diphthong로 이루어진다.

풀이 과정에서 어려운 점

- 정확하게 빈칸에 무엇을 어떻게 적어야 하는지 명확하지 않다. (문제 자체의 오류로 보임)
- 제시된 데이터의 강세위치와 발음기호를 알고 있어야 한다.

답안

a long vowel and one or multiple consonants after the core, a short vowel and multiple consonants after the core, a diphthong

과제

- rhyme의 heavy and light 개념을 정확하게 이해하자
- 명사, 형용사, 동사의 강세 패턴을 숙지하자.

2. 글 〈A〉를 읽고 강세규칙 (1)-①, (1)-②, (2)-①, (2)-②에 해당하는 단어의 기호를 〈B〉에서 각각 두 개씩 찾아 쓰시오. (단, 〈A〉에 제시된 강세규칙의 조건만을 고려할 것.) 【4 points】

2008-전국14

The rules of word stress placement in English are complex and have exceptions, but some information such as the grammatical category of the word, the number of syllables the word has, and the phonological structure of those syllables is important in stress placement. Consider the following stress placement rules:

(1) In three-syllable verbs,
① if the final syllable is strong, then it is stressed;
② if the final syllable is weak, then it is unstressed, and stress is placed on the preceding syllable if that syllable is strong.

(2) In three-syllable nouns,
① if the final syllable is weak, or ends with [aʊ], then it is unstressed; if the syllable preceding this final syllable is strong, then that middle syllable is stressed;
② if the second and third syllables are both weak, then the first syllable is stressed.

Note: A strong syllable has a rhyme which either has a syllable peak which is a long vowel or diphthong, or a vowel followed by a coda (i.e., one or more consonants). Weak syllables have a syllable peak which is a short vowel, and no coda unless the syllable peak is [ə].

(a) bonanza	(b) resurrect	(c) cinema	(d) remember
(e) embroider	(f) algebra	(g) entertain	(h) aroma

강세규칙	단어기호
(1)-①	(　　) (　　)
(1)-②	(　　) (　　)
(2)-①	(　　) (　　)
(2)-②	(　　) (　　)

출제 영역

Stress

출제 의도

동사와 명사의 강세 패턴에 따라 주어진 단어들의 강세위치를 파악할 수 있어야 한다.

문제 풀이 과정

A박스 요약 및 핵심내용

- 강세 패턴

(1) In three-syllable verbs,

① if the final syllable is strong, then it is stressed;

② if the final syllable is weak, then it is unstressed, and stress is placed on the preceding syllable if that syllable is strong.

(2) In three-syllable nouns,

① if the final syllable is weak, or ends with [aʊ], then it is unstressed; if the syllable preceding this final syllable is strong, then that middle syllable is stressed;

② if the second and third syllables are both weak, then the first syllable is stressed.

B박스 분석 과정

먼저 품사별로 분류하고 강세위치를 확인한다.

(1) 동사

① final syllable에 강세: (b) resurrect, (g) entertain

② second syllable에 강세: (d) remember, (e) embroider

(2) 명사

① second syllable에 강세: (a) bonanza, (h) aroma

② first syllable에 강세: (c) cinema, (f) algebra

풀이 과정에서 어려운 점

- 품사를 정확하게 구분해야 한다.
- 단어의 강세위치를 알고 있어야 한다.

답안

(1) ①: (b), (g)

②: (d), (e)

(2) ①: (a), (h)

②: (c), (f)

과제

- 동사, 명사, 형용사의 강세 패턴을 AEP를 참고하여 정리한다.
- AEP의 ch.7 Stress 부분에서 언급된 단어들의 강세위치를 숙지한다.

3. Read the passage in ⟨A⟩ and the examples in ⟨B⟩, and follow the directions. 【4 points】

2024-A6

When there are two or more feet in a word or phrase, in general, the rightmost foot gets a primary stress. Therefore, many English speakers would feel that 'teen' is stronger than 'four' in 'fourteen.' Another important tendency of English stress is that speech carries a regular alternation between stronger and weaker units. When 'fourteen men' is spoken in conversational style, the primary stress of 'fourteen' is adjusted. Since 'men' gets the primary stress of the whole phrase, 'four' is pronounced more strongly than 'teen' to avoid the clash of two lexical primary stresses.

(1) a. compact [ˌkʌmˈpækt]
   compact disk [ˈkʌmˌpækt ˈdɪsk]
 b. thirteenth [ˌθɜɹˈtinθ]
   thirteenth place [ˈθɜɹˌtinθ ˈpleɪs]
 c. good-looking [ˌgʊdˈlʊkɪŋ]
   good-looking tutor [ˈgʊdˌlʊkɪŋ ˈtjutəɹ]
 d. academic [ˌækəˈdɛmɪk]
   academic banter [ˈækəˌdɛmɪk ˈbæntəɹ]

As exemplified in (1), the secondary and the primary stresses of a word are reversed when it is followed by another word. This is called 'stress-shift' or 'rhythm reversal.'

Although English speakers have a strong tendency to use a regular rhythm in their speech, it is not the case that this stress-shift takes place whenever <u>the two feet containing a lexical primary stress are adjacent</u>. Look at the data in (2).

(2) a. maroon [məˈɹun]
   maroon sweater [məˈɹun ˈswɛtəɹ]
 b. away [əˈweɪ]
   away game [əˈweɪ ˈgeɪm]
 c. surrounding [səˈɹaʊndɪŋ]
   surrounding crowd [səˈɹaʊndɪŋ ˈkɹaʊd]
 d. dependent [dɪˈpɛndənt]
   dependent clause [dɪˈpɛndənt ˈklɔz]

a. maternal [məˈtɜɹnəl] love
b. economic [ˌɛkəˈnɑmɪk] growth
c. unexplained [ˌʌnɪkˈspleɪnd] symptom
d. approved [əˈpɹuvd] courses

Note: The phonetic forms given in ⟨B⟩ are the pronunciations of the first words when they are produced in isolation.

Based on ⟨A⟩, choose the TWO phrases where stress-shift can occur in ⟨B⟩. Then, besides the given phonological condition for stress-shift underlined in ⟨A⟩, state an additional phonological condition necessary for stress-shift.

출제 영역

Stress-shift or Rhythm reversal

출제 의도

stress-shift 현상을 이해하고 주어진 데이터를 분석 후 발생 환경을 기술할 수 있어야 한다.

문제 풀이 과정

A박스 요약 및 핵심내용

1. 'stress-shift' or 'rhythm reversal.' 현상

- When there are two or more feet in a word or phrase, in general, the rightmost foot gets a primary stress.
- Since 'men' gets the primary stress of the whole phrase, 'four' is pronounced more strongly than 'teen' to avoid the clash of two lexical primary stresses. ('fourteen man')

(1) a.	compact	[ˌkʌm'pækt]	(1)에서 첫 번째 단어가 secondary와 primary강세가 있어야 stress shift가 일어난다.
	compact disk	['kʌmˌpækt 'dɪsk]	
b.	thirteenth	[ˌθɜɹ'tinθ]	
	thirteenth place	['θɜɹˌtinθ 'pleɪs]	
c.	good-looking	[ˌgʊd'lʊkɪŋ]	
	good-looking tutor	['gʊdˌlʊkɪŋ 'tjutəɹ]	
d.	academic	[ˌækə'dɛmɪk]	
	academic banter	['ækəˌdɛmɪk 'bæntəɹ]	

2. stress-shift가 일어나지 않는 경우

It is not the case that this stress-shift takes place whenever the two feet containing a lexical primary stress are adjacent.

(2) a.	maroon	[mə'ɹun]	(2)에서 첫 번째 단어가 primary 강세만 있어 stress shift가 일어나지 않는다.
	maroon sweater	[mə'ɹun 'swɛtəɹ]	
b.	away	[ə'weɪ]	
	away game	[ə'weɪ 'geɪm]	
c.	surrounding	[sə'ɹaʊndɪŋ]	
	surrounding crowd	[sə'ɹaʊndɪŋ 'kɹaʊd]	
d.	dependent	[dɪ'pɛndənt]	
	dependent clause	[dɪ'pɛndənt 'klɔz]	

B박스 분석 과정

a. maternal [mə'tɜɹnəl] love → stress-shift 일어나지 않음
b. economic [ˌɛkə'nɑmɪk] growth → stress-shift 일어남
c. unexplained [ˌʌnɪk'spleɪnd] symptom → stress-shift 일어남
d. approved [ə'pɹuvd] courses → stress-shift 일어나지 않음

풀이 과정에서 어려운 점

- stress-shift 문제는 처음 출제됨. 따라서 심리적으로 어렵게 느껴짐

답안

Stress-shift can occur in the phrases (b) and (c). The following phonological condition for stress-shift should be added in ⟨A⟩ like 'a word containing a weak-strong sequence of feet (or secondary and primary stresses) and another foot are adjacent.

과제

'English Phonetics and Phonology'의 ch.9을 여러번 읽고 정리하자.

4. Read the passage in ⟨A⟩ and the examples in ⟨B⟩, and follow the directions. 【4 points】

2025-B04

Many word games in English rely on dominant stress patterns in English, in a way that if words do not meet phonological criteria on where stressed and unstressed syllables appear, they simply cannot be played. The name game, illustrated in the song The Name Game, is not an exception to this. Below are parts of the lyrics from the song, which show how the game is played with three common English names: Tony [tónɪ], Lana [lǽnə], and Kit [kít]. The phonetic transcription of the lyrics is provided below:

Tony, Tony, bo-bo-ney [tónɪ tónɪ bo bó ni]
Bo-na-na fana, fo-fo-ny [bə nǽ nə fǽnə fo fó ni]
Fee-fi-mo-mo-ney [fi faɪ mo mó ni]
To-ny [tó nɪ]

Lana, Lana bo-ba-na [lǽnə lǽnə bo bǽ nə]
Bo-na-na fana, fo-fa-na [bə nǽ nə fǽnə fo fǽ nə]
Fee-fi-mo-ma-na [fi faɪ mo mǽ nə]
La-na [lǽ nə]

Kit, Kit bo-bi-it [kít kít bo bí it]
Bo-na-na fana, fo-fi-it [bə nǽ nə fǽnə fo fí it]
Fee-fi-mo-mi-it [fi faɪ mo mí it]
Ki-it [kí it]

As shown in the lyrics above, the name game works with various names that consist of different segments or differ in length. However, some names are not permissible for the game, such as Jerome [ʤəɹóm], Michelle [mɪʃɛ́l], and Olivia[əlívɪə].

a. Annette [ənɛt]　　b. Miranda [məɹændə]
c. Nelson [nɛlsən]　　d. Pat [pæt]

Note: Some prosodic information has been intentionally left out for the names above.

Based on ⟨A⟩ , choose the TWO names in ⟨B⟩ that CANNOT be played for the name game. Then, state the prosodic condition necessary for names permissible for the game.

출제 영역

Stress

출제 의도

강세는 heavy한 음절에 위치할 수 있다는 간단한 규칙을 이름에 적용할 수 있는지 묻고 있다.

문제 풀이 과정

A박스 요약 및 핵심내용

1. 많은 word games이 강세패턴과 관련이 있다. 그중 하나가 'The Name Game'이다. Tony, Lana, Kit과 같은 이름들이 가능하다.
2. 'The Name Game'이 가능한 이름들은 단어의 segments나 단어 길이와는 관계없다. 하지만 불가능한 이름은 Jerome, Michelle, Olivia이다.

B박스 분석 과정

'The Name Game'이 가능한 이름(Tony, Lana, Kit)과 불가능한 이름(Jerome, Michelle, Olivia)의 운율적 차이를 비교하면 된다. 소리(segment)나 길이는 중요하지 않다고 했으니, 운율적 조건에서 강세(stress)와 음보(foot)가 주요 요소로 떠오를 것이다. 음보 조건이 배제되는 이유는 다음과 같다. 첫째, 지문의 첫 단락에서 '많은 word games이 강세 패턴과 관련이 있다'고 언급되었다. 둘째, 〈B〉박스에서 나타난 음보는 모두 강약(trochaic)격 음보를 보여준다. 예를 들어, Annette은 ə{nɛt}구조로, 첫 음절이 음보를 형성하지 못하고 두 번째 음절만 trochaic 음보 구조를 갖는다. Miranda도 마찬가지로 mə{ɹædə}형태의 trochaic 구조를 가진다. 따라서 운율적 조건으로 강세(stress) 위치를 언급해야 하며, 이름의 첫 번째 음절에 강세가 있는 이름만 가능하다.

풀이 과정에서 어려운 점

- 강세 문제를 처음 들어보는 'the Name Game'이란 게임에 연계해서 출제하다니! 너무 어색하다.

답안

(a) and (b) are not suitable for the name game. The prosodic condition necessary for the name game is that the primary stress must be on the first syllable of the name.

과제

이런 유형의 문제로 스트레스 받지 말고 욕 한 번 하고 넘어가자!

5. Read the passage and fill in the blanks. Write your answers in the correct order. 【2 points】 2016-A06

> English suffixes can be grouped into three different types when they are added to a root: stress-bearing, stress-shifting, and stress-neutral. Stress-bearing suffixes attract the primary stress to themselves as in (1a). Stress-shifting suffixes move the stress to some other syllables as in (1b). Stress-neutral suffixes do not make any difference to the stress of the root as in (1c). Meanwhile, the suffix -y is classified into two classes. Noun-forming suffix -y in (2) belongs to ______ suffixes, while adjective-forming suffix -y in (2) belongs to _______ suffixes.
>
> (1) a. engine-engineer, attest-attestation, statue-statuesque
> b. public-publicity, commerce-commercial, library-librarian
> c. clever-cleverness, consult-consultant, parent-parenthood
>
> (2) summer-summery, telephone-telephony,
> synonym-synonymy, frump-frumpy, advisor-advisory,
> photograph-photography, velvet-velvety

출제 영역

Stress 〉 Suffixes

출제 의도

Suffixes를 강세와 관련하여 세 가지 유형으로 분류하고 주어진 데이터를 통해 적용할 수 있어야 한다.

문제 풀이 과정

1. English suffixes 분류
   Stress-bearing suffixes attract the primary stress to themselves as in (1a).
   Stress-shifting suffixes move the stress to some other syllables as in (1b).
   Stress-neutral suffixes do not make any difference to the stress of the root as in (1c).

   (1) a. engine-engineer, attest-attestation, statue-statuesque
       b. public-publicity, commerce-commercial, library-librarian
       c. clever-cleverness, consult-consultant, parent-parenthood

2. Suffix -y 분류
   Noun-forming suffix -y : telephone-telephony, synonym-synonymy, photograph-photography
   Adjective-forming suffix -y : summer-summery, frump-frumpy, advisor-advisory, velvet-velvety

▶ 다른 하나는 -y가 첨가될 때 강세 변화의 유무이다. 변화가 있다면 형용사고 없다면 명사이다.

풀이 과정에서 어려운 점

- 풀이 과정은 단순하나 단어가 익숙치 않거나 강세 위치 파악이 어렵다면 부담스러울 수 있다. 특히 frumpy는 어려운 단어이다.

답안

stress-shifting, stress-neutral

과제

- 문제에서 언급된 단어들의 발음과 강세 위치를 정리한다.
- suffix를 derivational vs inflectional로 구분하는 내용을 정리하자.
- suffix를 class 1과 class 2로 분류하는 내용을 '이동걸 영어학2' 교재로 참고하여 정리하자.

6. Read ⟨A⟩ and ⟨B⟩ and answer the question. 【2.5 points】 2010-33

In English, some stress-shifting suffixes trigger a shift of stress in the base to which they are attached. In words with those suffixes, the assignment of stress depends on the syllabic internal structure of the base, as shown below: (1) The primary stress falls on the syllable that is immediately before the suffix if that syllable is heavy (e.g., súbstance – substántial) (2) If the syllable immediately before the suffix is light, the primary stress falls on the syllable immediately preceding that light syllable (e.g., admíre – ádmirable). (Note: A heavy syllable is defined as a syllable with a tense vowel, a diphthong, or a lax vowel followed by at least one coda segment. A light syllable, on the other hand, is an open syllable with one lax vowel, having no coda except when the vowel is /ə/.)

The suffixes are given in parentheses. a. homonym – homonymy (-y) b. context – contextual (-ual) c. navigate – navigation (-ion) d. compete – competency (-ency) e. insect – insecticide (-icide) f. advantage – advantageous (-eous)

Which of the following is the correct grouping for the data in ⟨B⟩ based on the rules of (1) and (2)?

	(1)	(2)
①	a, c, d	b, e, f
②	a, d, e	b, c, f
③	b, c	a, d, e, f
④	b, c, f	a, d, e
⑤	b, c, e, f	a, d

출제 영역

Stress 〉 Suffixes

출제 의도

Stress-shifting suffixes가 첨가될 때 base에 강세 변화가 발생한다. 지문에 제시된 규칙을 적용하여 제시된 data의 강세변화를 설명할 수 있어야 한다.

문제 풀이 과정

A박스 요약 및 핵심내용

1. Stress-shifting suffixes에서 강세위치 변화

the assignment of stress depends on the syllabic internal structure of the base, as shown below:

(1) The primary stress falls on the syllable that is immediately before the suffix if that syllable is heavy (e.g., súbstance – substántial)

(2) If the syllable immediately before the suffix is light, the primary stress falls on the syllable immediately preceding that light syllable (e.g., admíre – ádmirable).

B박스 분석 과정

강세위치를 통해 (1)에 속하는지 (2)에 속하는지 알 수 있다.

a. homonym – homonymy (-y) → 두 번째 음절에 강세 (2)
b. context – contextual (-ual) → 두 번째 음절에 강세 (1)
c. navigate – navigation (-ion) → 세 번째 음절에 강세 (1)
d. compete – competency (-ency) → 두 번째 음절에 강세 (2)
e. insect – insecticide (-icide) → 두 번째 음절에 강세 (1)
f. advantage – advantageous (-eous) → 두 번째 음절에 강세 (1)

풀이 과정에서 어려운 점

각 파생된 단어의 강세 위치를 알아야 한다.

답안

⑤

과제

문제에 제시된 단어들의 강세위치를 모두 정리한다.

CHAPTER

06

Foot

세부영역		출제년도	내용
1. Foot	1.1 개념	2005-전국18	How many feet?
	1.2 Trochaic	2021-A06	Preferred foot structure
	1.3 음운현상	2022-A06	Aspiration

❑ 연도별 출제빈도

2002	2003	2004	2005	2006	2007	2008	2009	2010	2011	2012	2013	2014	2015	2016	2017	2018	2019	2020	2021	2022	2023	2024	2025	2026
			*																*	*				?

1. 다음 <A>를 읽고, <B>가 특별한 강조나 대조없이 발음되었을 때, 몇 개의 음보(foot)로 이루어지는지 숫자로 쓰시오. 【3 points】 2005-전국18

Just as words have strong and weak parts, so do sentences have strong and weak parts. Function words are mostly unstressed in the sentence. English has stress-timed rhythm. There is neatly equal time between the sentence stresses. Stressed syllables will tend to occur at relatively regular intervals. Times from each stressed syllable to the next will tend to the same, irrespective of the number of intervening unstressed syllables. To express the notion of such rhythm, the foot is used as a unit of rhythm. The foot begins with a stressed syllable and includes all following unstressed syllables up to (but not including) the following stressed syllable.

Practice the sentences using natural rhythm and stress.

출제 영역

Foot

출제 의도

음보(foot)의 개념을 정확히 이해하고 제시된 data에서 foot단위를 구분할 수 있어야 한다.

문제 풀이 과정

A박스 요약 및 핵심내용

1. Stress-timed rhythm in English

There is neatly equal time between the sentence stresses. Stressed syllables will tend to occur at relatively regular intervals. Times from each stressed syllable to the next will tend to the same, irrespective of the number of intervening unstressed syllables.

2. Foot

The foot is used as a unit of rhythm. The foot begins with a stressed syllable and includes all following unstressed syllables up to (but not including) the following stressed syllable.

B박스 분석 과정

▶ foot정의에 따르면 foot단위는 강세음절 부터 그 다름 강세음절까지이다. 먼저 강세 위치를 알아야 한다. foot단위는 '{ }'로 표시한다. 아래 문장은 여섯 개의 foot으로 이루어졌다.

{Práctice the} {séntences} {úsing} {nátural} {rhýthm and} {stréss}.

풀이 과정에서 어려운 점

foot단위는 강세받는 음절이 기준이므로 강세받는 음절의 위치를 정확하게 알아야 한다.

답안

6 feet

과제

foot과 관련된 문제가 최근에 많이 출제되므로 'EPP' ch.9 참고하여 정리해 두자.

2. Read the passage and follow the directions. 【4 points】 2021-A06

'Foot' is a prosodic unit above syllable, which consists of one obligatory strong syllable and optional weak syllables. Feet seem to have many different structures in English. For example, there are feet composed of a single stressed syllable (e.g., {'son}) and feet where a stressed syllable is followed by one stressless syllable (e.g., {'mother}) or by two or more stressless syllables (e.g., {'Canada}). Sometimes, a strong syllable appears in the second (e.g., {de'mand), {ba'nana}).

Foot structure can change due to [ə]-deletion. First, the data in (1) show that [ə] in an initial stressless syllable can be deleted in fast speech.

(1)	Normal speech	Fast speech
a. Toronto	[tʰə'rantoʊ]	['tr̥antoʊ]
b. Marina	[mə'rinə]	['mrinə]

Second, the data in (2) demonstrate that [ə] in a medial stressless syllable can be deleted after a stressed and before a stressless syllable in fast speech.

(2)	Normal speech	Fast speech
a. opera	['apərə]	['aprə]
b. general	['ʤenərəl]	['ʤenrəl]

Third, the data in (3) tell us that when two stressless syllables occur between two stressed syllables, [ə] in either stressless syllable can be deleted in fast speech.

(3)	Normal speech	Fast speech
a. respiratory	['rɛspərəˌtʰəri]	['rɛsprəˌtʰəri] or ['rɛspərˌtʰɔri]
b. glorification	[ˌglərəfə'kʰeɪʃən]	[ˌglərfə'kʰeɪʃən] or [ˌglərəf'kʰeɪʃən]

However, [ə]-deletion cannot occur even in fast speech when a stressless syllable occurs directly between two stressed syllables as in (4).

(4)	Normal speech	Fast speech
a. operatic	[ˌapə'ræɾɪk]	[ˌapə'ræɾɪk], *[ˌap'ræɾɪk]
b. generality	[ˌʤɛnə'ræləɾi]	[ˌʤɛnə'ræləɾi], *[ˌʤɛn'ræləɾi]

Note 1: indicates a non-permissible form.
Note 2: "indicates foot boundaries.

a respirate ['rɛspəˌreɪt] b. chocolate ['ʧakəlɪt]
c. nationalize ['næʃənəˌlaɪz] d. glorify ['glɔrəˌfaɪ]

Based on ⟨A⟩, identify TWO words in ⟨B⟩ where [ə] can be deleted in fast speech. Then, describe the foot structure that is most preferred in fast speech, based on ⟨A⟩

출제 영역 Foot

출제 의도

음보의 구조를 이해하고 선호되는 음보 구조를 유지하기 위해 어떤 현상이 일어나는지 말할 수 있어야 한다.

문제 풀이 과정

A박스 요약 및 핵심내용

1. Trochaic foot 구조
   a. a single stressed syllable (e.g., {'son})
   b. a stressed syllable is followed by one stressless syllable (e.g., {'mother})
   c. a stressed syllable is followed by two or more stressless syllables (e.g., {'Canada}).
   d. a strong syllable appears in the second (e.g., {de'mand), {ba'nana}).
2. [ə]-deletion으로 인한 foot구조 변화
   - [ə] in an initial stressless syllable can be deleted in fast speech.

(1)	Normal speech	Fast speech	
a. Toronto	[tʰə'rantoʊ]	['trantoʊ]	a. SWW → SW 으로 변화
b. Marina	[mə'rinə]	['mrinə]	b. WSW → SW 으로 변화

   - [ə] in a medial stressless syllable can be deleted after a stressed and before a stressless syllable in fast speech.

(2)	Normal speech	Fast speech	
a. opera	['apərə]	['aprə]	a. SWW → SW 으로 변화
b. general	['ʤenərəl]	['ʤenrəl]	b. SWW → SW 으로 변화

   - When two stressless syllables occur between two stressed syllables, [ə] in either stressless syllable can be deleted in fast speech.

(3)	Normal speech	Fast speech	첫 번째 음보의 변화
a. respiratory	['rɛspərə,tʰəri]	['rɛsprə,tʰəri] or ['rɛspər,tʰɔri]	a. SWW → SW 으로 변화
b. glorification	[,glərəfə'kʰeɪʃən]	[,glərfə'kʰeɪʃən] or [,glərəf'kʰeɪʃən]	b. SWW → SW 으로 변화

3. [ə]-deletion이 일어나지 않는 경우
   - [ə]-deletion cannot occur when a stressless syllable occurs directly between two stressed syllables.

(4)	Normal speech	Fast speech
a. operatic	[,apə'ræɾɪk]	[,apə'ræɾɪk], *[,ap'ræɾɪk]
b. generality	[,ʤɛnə'rælərí]	[,ʤɛnə'rælərí], *[,ʤɛn'rælərí]

B박스 분석 과정

1. [ə] deletion 일어나는 단어? (4)의 *[,ap'ræɾɪk], *[,ʤɛn'rælərí]에서 왜 일어나지 않는지 분석해야 한다.
   ▶ 강세음절 바로 뒤에 강세받지 않는 음절이 오지 않았기 때문이다. [ə]삭제 해도 'SW'구조를 유지한다면 삭제가 일어나고 그렇지 않다면 삭제될 수 없다.

   a respirate ['rɛspə,reɪt], b. chocolate ['ʧakəlɪt], c. nationalize ['næʃənə,laɪz], d. glorify ['glɔrə,faɪ]

2. foot structure that is most preferred in fast speech, based on 〈A〉?
   ▶ [ə]삭제로 인한 음보의 변화와 [ə]삭제가 될 수 없는 이유를 살펴보라. {SW}음보 구조를 유지하려는 경향이 있다.

풀이 과정에서 어려운 점

(4)에서 [ə]삭제가 일어나지 않는 이유와 선호하는 foot구조를 찾아내는 과정이 어렵다.

답안

[ə] in the words (b) and (c) can be deleted in fast speech. The foot structure in which a stressed syllable is followed by one stressless syllable is most preferred in fast speech.

3. Read the passage and follow the directions. 【4 points】 2022-A06

In English, prosodic units such as syllable and foot are referred to in the phonological description. Here we are going to refer to foot, which is trochaic in English as in (1).

(1) a. di{ˈsaster} sy{ˈnopsis} mi{ˈmosa}
b. {ˈopportune} {ˈinsolent} {ˈenmity}
c. {ˌresur}{ˈrect} {ˌphoto}{ˈgraphic} {ˌeco}{ˈnomical}

Now take a look at the data in (2). Voiceless stops are aspirated when they are followed by a stressed vowel, whether it is a primary stress as in (2a) or a secondary stress asin (2b). But even before a stressed vowel, they are not aspirated when it is preceded by /s/ as in (2c). Lastly, they are not aspirated when they are followed by an unstressed vowel as in (2d). So the phonological description of the aspiration phenomenon must be complicated without referring to foot.

(2)	a.	apartment	[əˈpʰɑɹtmənt]
		maternal	[məˈtʰɜɹnəl]
		academy	[əˈkʰædəmi]
	b.	personality	[ˌpʰɜɹsəˈnæləti]
		Tennessee	[ˌtʰɛnəˈsi]
		kangaroo	[ˌkʰæŋgəˈɹu]
	c.	asparagus	[əˈspæɹəgəs]
		austerity	[ɔˈstɛɹəti]
		mosquito	[məˈskitoʊ]
	d.	sympathy	[ˈsɪmpəθi]
		sentimental	[ˌsɛntəˈmɛntəl]
		alcoholic	[ˌælkəˈhɔlɪk]

Note: '{ }' indicates foot boundaries.

a. operation b. disentangle c. accountability d. substantial

In ⟨A⟩, select TWO words where the underlined voiceless stop is realized as an aspirated stop. Then, state a rule which can account for all the aspirated stops in (2). Your answer must include 'foot.'

출제 영역

Foot & Aspiration

출제 의도

음보(foot)구조와 대기음화(aspiration)현상을 이해하고 대기음화 현상을 foot단위에 기초해서 설명할 수 있어야 한다.

문제 풀이 과정

A박스 요약 및 핵심내용

1. Trochaic foot stucture

(1) a. di{'saster} sy{'nopsis} mi{'mosa}
b. {'opportune} {'insolent} {'enmity}
c. {ˌresur}{'rect} {ˌphoto}{'graphic} {ˌeco}{'nomical}

2. Aspiration 현상

- Aspiration 일어남

(2) a. apartment [ə'{pʰɑɹtmənt}], maternal [mə{'tʰɜɹnəl}], academy [ə'{kʰædəmi}]
b. personality [{ˌpʰɜɹsə}{'næləti}], Tennessee [{ˌtʰɛnə}{'si}], kangaroo [{ˌkʰæŋgə}{'ɹu}]

- Aspiration 일어나지 않음

c. asparagus [ə'{spæɹəgəs}], austerity [ɔ'{stɛɹəti}], mosquito [mə{'skitoʊ}]
d. sympathy [{'sɪmpəθi}], sentimental [{ˌsɛntə}{'mɛntəl}], alcoholic [{ˌælkə}{'hɔlɪk}]

▶ (2a,b)와 (2c,d)의 foot구조를 비교해 봐야 한다. foot구조는 '{ }'표시한다. Aspirated stops가 포함된 foot을 보면 모두 foot initial position에 위치한다. 하지만 그렇지 않은 경우는 foot initial position에 위치하지 않는다.

B박스 분석 과정

1. 대기음화 현상이 일어나는 단어 찾기

a. {ope}{ration} b. {disen}{tangle} c. a{ccounta}{bility} d. sub{stantial}

▶ 음보 단위로 구분하고 foot initial position에 위치하는지 확인한다. 이 때 단어의 강세위치를 정확하게 알아야 한다. (b)와 (c)에서 stop이 foot initial position에 위치한다.

풀이 과정에서 어려운 점

기존의 aspiration현상에 대한 설명, 즉 '강세받는 음절의 onset position에 위치하고 /s/가 앞에 없을 때'라는 환경대신에 foot단위를 사용해서 설명하는 것이 낯설고 어렵게 느껴질 수 있다.

답안

The voiceless stops in (b) and (c) are realized as aspirated stops. Voiceless stops are aspirated when they occur in the initial position of a trochaic foot.

과제

대기음화 현상을 strong aspirated, weak aspirated, unaspirated로 구분하고 각 환경을 설명하는 내용을 AEP를 참고하여 정리하자.

CHAPTER

07

Intonation

세부영역		출제년도	내용
1. Intonation	1.1 Tonic Accent	2008-서울인천06	Intonation
		2005-전국23	Tonic Accent
		2004-전국09	Intonation (falling)

❑ 연도별 출제빈도

2002	2003	2004	2005	2006	2007	2008	2009	2010	2011	2012	2013	2014	2015	2016	2017	2018	2019	2020	2021	2022	2023	2024	2025	2026
		*	*			*																		?

1. 다음 발음에 관한 〈A〉와 〈B〉를 읽고, 〈B〉의 밑줄 그은 부분에 알맞은 말을 쓰시오.
【3 points】 2004-전국09

대화 상황:

A foreign student is applying for a library card at a university library. He is handed a form by an overworked male assistant, who is a native speaker of English, but after looking at it, he realized it is the wrong one.

대화:

Foreign student:	Excuse ↘ME. You have ↘GIVEn me the ↘↘WRONG form.
Library assistant:	Sorry, I gave you what you ↘ASKed for [irritated, appeals to others in the queue for support].
Foreign student:	↘↘No, It ↘IS the ↘↘WRONG form.
Library assistant:	OK. There's no need to be rude.

Key: ↘means falling intonation.
↘↘ means extra emphasis on stressed syllables.
Capital letters mean stressed syllables.

Instead of the underlined section of the conversation, a native speaker of English might say the following:
"Ex↘CUSE me. You've given me the wrong ↘FORM."
Compared to the native speaker's utterance, the foreign student's pronunciation appears to give the impression of being ________.

출제 영역

Intonation

출제 의도

출제 의도가 현재 출제 유형과 전혀 다름. 그래서 분석할 필요 없음.

문제 풀이 과정

풀이 과정에서 어려운 점

답안

rude

과제

2. 다음 〈A〉를 읽고, 〈B〉가 나타내고자 하는 의미를 "as well as"를 사용하여 한 문장의 영어로 쓰시오. (문장에서 진한 글씨체로 된 부분은 억양구에서 엑센트(tonic accent)를 받는 곳임)

2005-전국23

The position of a tonic accent is closely connected with information type. A focused constituent usually receives the tonic accent, while a non-focused constituent, which is understood to be old information or is presupposed, is unaccented. Consider the following sentence:

Peter met Jennifer in his office, too.

The meaning of *too* is to indicate that what has been said previously with the use of one word or term applies as well with the use of another word of the same form-class. For example, if *Jennifer* and *too* are accented in this sentence (/Peter met Jennifer in his office, //too./), it is presupposed that Peter met some other person in his office and the presupposed part is unaccented. Thus, the sentence means that Peter met Jennifer as well as some other person.

/ Peter met Jennifer in his office, // too./

출제 영역

Intonation

출제 의도

억양구에 tonic accent를 받는것과 정보유형의 관계를 이해하고, 'too'의 기능도 이해한 후 주어진 문장의 의미를 말할 수 있어야 한다.

문제 풀이 과정

A박스 요약 및 핵심내용

1. Tonic accent와 information type의 관계

A focused constituent usually receives the tonic accent, while a non-focused constituent, which is understood to be old information or is presupposed, is unaccented.

Peter met Jennifer in his office, too.

2. 'too'의 의미

The meaning of *too* is to indicate that what has been said previously with the use of one word or term applies as well with the use of another word of the same form-class.

(/Peter met Jennifer in his office, //too./)

의미: Peter met Jennifer as well as some other person.

B박스 분석 과정

▶ 'Peter'가 tonic accent를 받으므로 새로운 정보라는 의미이다. 따라서 Peter외에 다른 사람도 Jennifer를 만났다는 의미이다. 참고로 '/ /'는 억양구 단위를 표시한다.

/Peter met Jennifer in his office,// too./

풀이 과정에서 어려운 점

Tonic accent의 기능과 too의 의미관계를 연계해서 이해해야 하는 점이 어렵다.

답안

Peter as well as some other person met Jennifer in his office.

과제

- AEP의 ch.7의 7.8 Intonation 부분을 읽고 정리하자.
- tonic accent, tonic syllable, intonational phrase 용어를 정리하자.

3. 다음 글을 읽고, 지시에 따르시오. 【4 points】 2008-서울인천06

> Intonation in question functions to differentiate normal information from contrastive or expressive intentions. In order words, intonation performs an important conversation management function, with the speaker being able to subtly signal to the interlocutor to respond in a particular fashion, or to pay particular attention to a piece of highlighted information.
>
> There are two syntactic options for making yes/no questions. The first option, which is general or unmarked, involves the inversion of the subject and the auxiliary verb, as in (1).
>
> (1) Did Tom cook DINner?
>
> This unmarked option is accompanied by rising intonation. In this pattern, the speaker is asking about the truth of what he or she saying.
>
> The second option, which is less general or marked, takes the form of a statement with no subject-auxiliary inversion, as in (2).
>
> (2) Tom cooked DINner?
>
> In this marked pattern with rising intonation, the speaker is either asking the interlocutor to repeat or is making an assumption and wants the interlocutor to confirm it (i.e., the speaker has good reason to expect a yes answer.)
>
> Another prosodic pattern for the uninverted question has emphatic stress, high pitch, and exaggerated intonation on one or two of the constituents that lend themselves to focus, as in (3).
>
> (3) TOM cooked DINner?
>
> In this pattern, the speaker is reacting with surprise or disbelief to certain information just received.
>
> For learners of English, it does not make sense to practice the unmarked and marked versions of *Tom cooked dinner* in isolation and out of context. Learners must understand early on that one version is appropriate in one context, whereas the other is appropriate in another context.

아래 대화의 빈칸 (1)에 들어갈 kelly의 발화를 위 글 (1)-(3)에서 찾아 번호를 쓰고, 대화의 내용에 근거하여 그 이유를 50자 내외의 우리말로 쓰시오.

> (Kelly is a friend of Lisa's family.)
> Lisa: The guys kept doing nice things for me because it was Mother's Day. Bob washed the car, Joe ironed the shirts, and Tom cooked dinner.
> Kelly: (1)______________________
> Lisa: It was quite amazing to me, too. He's never even boiled an egg before.

출제 영역

Intonation과 Yes/no questions

출제 의도

intonation pattern이 다른 다양한 yes/no questions을 이해하고 제시된 상황에 적절한 yes/no question을 찾을 수 있어야 한다.

문제 풀이 과정

A박스 요약 및 핵심내용

1. Function of Intonation:
To differentiate normal information from contrastive or expressive intentions.

2. yes/no questions의 두 가지 유형과 기능
a. the inversion of the subject and the auxiliary verb and accompanied by rising intonation. In this pattern, the speaker is asking about the truth of what he or she saying.

(1) Did Tom cook DINner?

b. takes the form of a statement with no subject-auxiliary inversion, with rising intonation. Asking the interlocutor to repeat or is making an assumption and wants the interlocutor to confirm it

(2) Tom cooked DINner?

Another prosodic pattern for the uninverted question has emphatic stress, high pitch, and exaggerated intonation on one or two of the constituents that lend themselves to focus. In this pattern, the speaker is reacting with surprise or disbelief to certain information just received.

(3) TOM cooked DINner?

B박스 분석 과정

▶ Lisa의 마지막 발화내용을 통해 Kelly도 Tom의 행동에 매우 놀랐다는 것을 알 수 있다. 따라서 화자가 특정 정보에 surprise or disbelief를 보이는 형태는 (3)이다.

풀이 과정에서 어려운 점

답안

(3); The reason Kelly responded to what Lisa said is that Kelly was surprised or in disbelief to the fact that Tom cooked dinner because he never did so before.

과제

- AEP의 ch.7의 7.8 Intonation 부분을 읽고 정리하자.
- tonic accent, tonic syllable, intonational phrase 용어를 정리하자.

재미와 실력을 동시에,

중등영어

이동걸 영어학

기출문제분석

통사론+음운론

초판 1쇄 발행 2025년 07월 25일

저자 이동걸
발행인 공태현 **발행처** (주)법률저널
등록일자 2008년 9월 26일 **등록번호** 제15-605호
주소 151-862 서울 관악구 복은4길 50 (서림동 120-32)
대표전화 02)874-1144 **팩스** 02)876-4312
홈페이지 www.lec.co.kr
ISBN 979-11-7384-045-6 (13740)
정가 20,000원